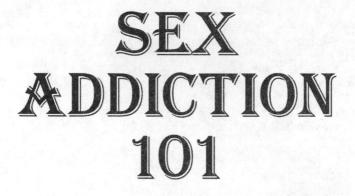

SEX ADDICTION 101

A BASIC GUIDE TO HEALING FROM SEX, PORN, AND LOVE ADDICTION

ROBERT WEISS, MSW

D0064567

Health Communications, Inc.
Deerfield Beach, Florida

www.hcibooks.com

Library of Congress Cataloging-in-Publication Data
is available through the Library of Congress

ISBN-13: 978-07573-1843-6 (Paperback)
ISBN-10: 07573-1843-6 (Paperback)
ISBN-13: 978-07573-1844-3 (ePub)
ISBN-10: 07573-1844-4 (ePub)

Publisher: Health Communications, Inc.
    3201 S.W. 15th Street
    Deerfield Beach, FL 33442–8190

Cover and interior design by Lawna Patterson Oldfield

CONTENTS

Additional material, worksheets, and writing exercises may be found by visiting
www.hcibooks.com.

ACKNOWLEDGMENTS

This book is dedicated to those individuals (below) who pioneered and persevered in the early research and treatment of addictive sexual and intimacy disorders. If not for *each one of you*, this book would never have been written, nor would I still be alive to write it. *Sex Addiction 101* is a summation of your commitment to sound ideas and solid research. Thus, this book belongs to all of you, as well as to the reader. You are the pioneering researchers; writers and therapists who risked your professional reputations and careers to help all of us make sense of this shameful, hidden, emotional disorder (compulsive, addictive, non-offending sexual behavior).

Even when surrounded by professional arrogance, dismissal, and derision, you fearlessly beat back the bushes of cultural prejudice and fear, offering hope to people who surely had none. You constantly discussed the issues that no one wanted to discuss and you never stopped talking about them, even when it was uncomfortable or out of fashion. By standing firm in your truth, each of you have helped even the most shamed addict hold out hope that their life might have genuine worth and value—regardless of their prior history. And I am one of those people. Thus, I am personally and professionally forever in all of your debt. As are the tens of thousands of recovering people whose lives are now forever changed for the better because you stood up for them when no one else would.

This book is dedicated to:

Ken Adams	Al Cooper
Jennifer Schneider	Michael Seto
Patrick Carnes	David Delmonico
Wendy Maltz	Charlotte Kasl
Brenda Schaffer	Eli Coleman
Ralph Earle	Marty Kafka
Mark Laaser	

Thank you. Each of you has contributed to making our world a better place.

AUTHOR'S NOTE

This is not a book about morality, cultural beliefs, cultural norms, or religion. It is not written as a challenge to those who enjoy recreational sexuality or "nontraditional" sexuality, either casually or as a lifestyle. As a mental health and addiction professional, it is not my job to judge such behaviors in any way. Instead, I have written this book to help people whose sexual fantasies and activities have run amok to the point where they've become a driving life force—overriding their personal goals, beliefs, and lifestyle. In other words, this book is written for those whose abusive and/or addictive involvement with objectified, often nonintimate sexuality, consistently and persistently distracts them from larger personal goals like academic achievement, career development, intimate relationships, recreation, emotional health, and community. Within these pages, I offer understanding, compassion, direction, and hope to those who are too ashamed, fearful, or embarrassed to reach out in other ways.

Although there are many views about whether things like pornography, virtual sex, casual/anonymous sex, and nontraditional sex are right or wrong, good or bad, moral or immoral, it is not the intent of this book to define or address these issues in any meaningful way. I support every adult in his or her right to engage in any solo or mutually consensual (and legal) sexual activity or experience that provides pleasure, satisfaction, and fulfillment. I do not believe that anyone, therapist or not, has the right to judge what turns someone on or how a person pursues sexual activity—as long as that person's choices do not violate the intrinsic rights and safety of self or others. In short, my work is not focused on what is ethically or politically correct for any individual or the culture at large. With pornography, for instance, I do not promote censorship, nor do I believe that all porn is automatically problematic or exploitative, though some (child porn, for instance) certainly can be.

My primary goal is to assist people who struggle with compulsive and addictive sexual behaviors by helping them to identify their problem as the chronic emotional disorder it is, and to then understand that the problem can be put into remission with proper care and direction—just like alcoholism, compulsive gambling, eating disorders, and/or drug addiction. In a nutshell, I want those who are suffering from sexual addiction to know that their sexual concerns can be addressed without shame or moral/cultural/religious bias. I also seek to offer direction and insight to therapists who may be unfamiliar with the treatment of sexually addicted clients. But most of all, I want to offer sex addicts hope, letting them know that long-term change and healing are possible to anyone willing to invest in the hard work of personal growth and integrity.

—*Robert Weiss, LCSW, CSAT-S*

FOREWORD

Mention "sex addiction" and most people's response is, "Sounds fun. Where do I sign up?" In reality, however, sexual addiction is as devastatingly un-fun as a full-blown addiction to alcohol, crystal meth, heroin, and/or any other intensely pleasurable and/or dissociative high. All of these behaviors (sex included) typically start out as a good time, and many people who engage in them feel great . . . for a while. But among those individuals who struggle with underlying emotional or psychological issues such as profound childhood or adult trauma, anxiety, depression, and low self-esteem the tide will eventually turn, and instead of *wanting* alcohol, drugs, sex, gaming, and/or to binge eat they end up *needing* alcohol, drugs, sex, gaming and/or binge eating—just to feel okay. Before they even realize it, they're "feeding the beast," drinking, using, or acting out, not to get high with friends, party, and have a great time, but to escape the pain of living life on life's terms.

People often ask me, "How can someone be addicted to sex?" They may as well be asking, "How can a person be addicted to *any* behavior? Don't you have to put a substance into your body to experience the euphoric rush that drives addiction?" My answer to these and similar questions is usually something along the lines of: "In the world of addiction treatment there are two major areas of concern— addiction to substances, and addiction to patterns of behavior. Typically, substance addictions involve abuse of and dependency upon chemicals such as alcohol, nicotine, prescription drugs, and illegal drugs like heroin, meth, or cocaine, whereas behavioral addictions, also known as "process addictions," are problematic, repetitive behavior patterns involving potentially pleasurable or compulsive activities such as gambling, sex, working, spending, eating, etc." Then I explain the ways in which addictive substances *and behaviors* affect the human brain.

The Brain on Drugs vs. the Brain on Sex

Much of the confusion around what constitutes a "process addiction" centers on the fact that many potentially addictive behaviors are healthy, even essential activities with which the majority of the population has little concern or personal struggle. In fact, things like eating and sex contribute to both individual survival and survival of the species, so our brains are programmed to encourage participation in these activities. That encouragement arrives when these behaviors trigger a dopamine response in the rewards center of the brain, resulting in feelings of pleasure. Alcohol and addictive drugs cause a similar neural response. In fact, imaging studies show that the brain on cocaine and the brain when sexually aroused are virtually indistinguishable. In other words, the human brain reacts to sex the same way it reacts to cocaine—one of the most highly addictive substances known to man.

Not surprisingly, this neurochemical pleasure process is a key element in the development and maintenance of addictions, be they substance or behavioral. Individuals struggling with underlying emotional or psychological issues subconsciously learn to abuse the brain's dopamine response via a substance or pleasurable activity *as a means of coping with stress and/or masking emotional pain*. Repeatedly using a substance or pleasurable behavior in this way teaches the brain that the way to feel better is to ingest more of that substance or engage in more of that behavior. So whatever the addictive substance or behavior, the drive is the same—addicts want to *feel better*, which usually means *feeling less*, and they know their addiction is the easiest way to (temporarily) disconnect, numb out, and not have to experience the difficulties of life.

The Downside of Sex Addiction

Sexual addiction, like all addictions, is not all fun and games. It has a definite downside. To understand this downside we first must understand what, exactly, sexual addiction is. As my esteemed colleague Rob Weiss writes:

SEXUAL ADDICTION, ALSO KNOWN AS "hypersexuality" or "hyper-sexual disorder," is a dysfunctional preoccupation with sexual fantasy and behavior, often involving the obsessive pursuit of non-intimate sex, pornography, compulsive masturbation, romantic intensity, and objectified partner sex. This adult obsessive pattern of thoughts and behaviors continues for a period of at least six months, despite the following:

1) Attempts made to self-correct the problematic sexual behavior

2) Promises made to self and others to change the sexual behavior

3) Significant, directly related negative life consequences such as relationship instability, emotional turmoil, physical health problems, career trouble, and legal issues

In other words, sex addicts have lost control over their sexual behavior, they are unable to stop their sexual acting out even when they want to, and they experience *significant, directly related negative life consequences*. (This is a pretty good definition for *any* addiction.)

For now, I want to focus on the last part—the consequences of sexual addiction. Most sex addicts are deeply ashamed of their behavior and who wouldn't be? Because of this they most often find themselves leading a double life: keeping their sexual acting out a secret from family and friends, and separating what they do sexually from the rest of their day-to-day life. This compartmentalization leads to the creation of an ever-expanding web of lies told to both self and others. Typically it is the lying, secrecy, and lack of personal integrity that cause the most pain to not only the addict, but also the addict's spouse or partner (if he or she is in a committed relationship). There are other consequences as well. Hours spent compulsively masturbating to online pornography or pursuing potential sex partners on dating or social media sites and apps are hours not spent developing one's career, nurturing one's spouse and/or children, hanging out with friends, enjoying hobbies, and engaging in various other necessary forms of self-care. Furthermore, sex addicts who act out with others (not all sex addicts do) are at a much higher than normal risk of contracting sexually transmitted diseases, including HIV. And the behavior of some sex addicts eventually escalates into illegal activities such as public sex, exhibitionism, voyeurism, illegal forms of pornography, etc., resulting in arrest, public humiliation, and possibly even incarceration.

Addiction Hopping

As any recovering addict can tell you, fighting addiction sometimes feels like playing an endless game of Whack-A-Mole, the carnival game where you pound on plastic moles whenever and wherever they pop up, only to spot various other moles rising from their holes. No matter how many moles you hammer down, another one seems to appear. Addiction is the same way, except the moles that pop up are cross-addictions (meaning the addict uses one addiction to replace another) or co-occurring disorders (meaning two disorders are present at the same time). Whack down booze, and food or nicotine pops up. In fact, it's quite common to see newly sober alcoholics gaining a quick twenty pounds, and long-ago ex smokers opening up a fresh pack almost immediately after they stop drinking.

Needless to say, addiction's "moles" come in an almost endless variety. A few weeks ago I performed a quick online search of the *New York Times* using the word "addiction" to see how many options would be listed. In the preceding month, addiction had been used to describe: numerous drugs both legal and illegal, alcohol, smoking, gambling, spending, political spending, fame, horses, preservation of natural resources, smartphones, and Facebook. And those were just the then-topical offerings. Not mentioned during that period were many of the normally newsworthy addictions like work, sugar, binging, purging, shopping, exercising, relationships, and sex.

At the various chemical addiction treatment centers operated by my corporation, Elements Behavioral Health, clients arrive seeking help with alcohol, prescription drugs, and/or illicit drugs. We subsequently find that nearly all of them also suffer from at least one cross- or co-occurring addiction, the three most common of which are: nicotine, eating, and sex. For addicts at our sexual addiction treatment centers—in other words, *addicts for whom sex is the primary problem*—the story is the same. We see these individuals time and time again turning to nicotine, food, alcohol, or drugs as a replacement for their sexual acting out. These "related addictions" are so prevalent that at Elements facilities we now actively seek to identify and address cross- and co-occurring issues during the first thirty days of treatment. These disorders are nothing new, of course, but addressing them early in recovery certainly is.

Why This Book?

Much has been written about sexual addiction in the last thirty years. The onslaught began with Patrick Carnes' groundbreaking work, *Out of the Shadows: Understanding Sexual Addiction*, published in 1983. Prior to that, clinicians were "diagnosing" excessive consensual adult sexual behavior patterns using antiquated, pejorative terms like "nymphomania" and "Don Juan-ism." Hardly anyone back then had even the faintest idea of what sexual addiction really was, how to diagnose it, its devastating effects, and how to treat it. Even now there is a great deal of confusion, even within the therapeutic community, with some well meaning "sex-positive" clinicians actually arguing there is no such thing as sexual addiction. (The majority of those clinicians, if pressed, will nonetheless concede that some people do struggle with impulsive and compulsive sexual acting out. These therapists' bone of contention seems to center on using the potentially sex-negative word "addiction" in describing such activity.)

Beyond the controversy over nomenclature (how we name this problem) there remains considerable confusion surrounding the identification, effects of, and treatment of sexual addiction. In truth, very few therapists possess a comprehensive understanding of this incredibly complicated disease, and of those individuals only a handful can present that information in words accessible to the layperson. Among these rare individuals is Rob Weiss, an early protégé of Patrick Carnes. In 1995 Rob founded the Sexual Recovery Institute in Los Angeles, one of the first facilities anywhere offering treatment for sexual addiction and related issues. These days Rob is Senior Vice President of Clinical Development, overseeing the development of

addiction and mental health programs at multiple treatment programs around the United States. Additionally, he provides sexual
addiction treatment training internationally for psychology professionals, addiction treatment centers, and the US military. He has
been featured on CNN, *Today*, the *Daily Beast*, the *Oprah Network*,
ESPN and in the *Wall Street Journal* among many other media outlets internationally. In many ways today, along with his mentor Patrick Carnes, Rob has become the face of and driving force behind
understanding and treating profound intimacy disorders like sexual
addiction.

Since *Out of the Shadows* first appeared literally dozens of books
on sexual addiction have been published, but hardly any present the
comprehensive overview found herein, and none are as up-to-date.
This book covers everything from what sexual addiction is and how it
can best be treated, to how it affects various subgroups of the population such as women, gays, and teenagers, to how sex addicts can protect themselves from the online sexual onslaught. And Rob presents
this material in straightforward, concise language that any reader can
understand. Clearly, this work is intended to enlighten not only the
clinical population, but actual sex addicts and those who love them.
If you are a therapist, my sincere hope is that you will find something
here that helps you to help others, and if you are a sex addict or the
partner thereof, my hope is that you will come away with a better
understanding of this complicated issue, and also with some useful
ideas on how to overcome this very serious addiction.

—*David Sack, MD*

1

Defining Sexual Addiction

BOB IS A THIRTY-SIX-YEAR-OLD DIVORCED financial analyst. His wife left him twelve years ago after she learned that he'd been cheating on her with multiple women the entire eleven months they were married and most of the two years prior to that, when they were dating and engaged. After the divorce, without the constraints of marriage, casual sex with any willing woman became Bob's top priority—not that it hadn't been already. In the beginning, most of his "work" was done in bars and clubs. As time progressed, however, his behaviors moved more into the online realm. He found that video chat sites provided access to a lot more women than a local nightclub, and that most of those women were online for the same reason he was: casual sex. Eventually he discovered hookup apps like Blendr, Tinder, and Ashley Madison. "Those were like crack cocaine," he says. With the apps, he was suddenly having sex with multiple women weekly. In time, of course, his work suffered, his friendships suffered, and he grew increasingly anxious, short-tempered, and depressed. Finally, he went to a therapist seeking treatment for his depression, and described his life. A lightbulb went off when the clinician said, "You know, I think you might have an issue with sexual addiction." Before that, the idea had never even crossed Bob's mind. He just thought he was a "ladies' man." But when his therapist said the words *sexual addiction*, he knew it was true.

What Makes an Addiction an Addiction?

Before discussing the specifics of sex addiction, it may be helpful to briefly define addiction in general terms. Put simply, the criteria for addiction (of all types) are as follows:

✓ Preoccupation to the point of obsession with the substance or behavior of choice
✓ Loss of control over use of the substance or behavior, typically evidenced by failed attempts to quit or cut back
✓ Directly related negative consequences: relationship trouble, issues at work or in school, declining physical health, depression, anxiety, diminished self-esteem, isolation, financial woes, loss of interest in previously enjoyable activities, legal trouble, etc.

Today, most people readily understand the concept of substance addiction. If they have not been addicted themselves (to cigarettes, alcohol, prescription medications, illicit drugs, etc.), then they probably know someone who is. Or, at the very least, they've seen relatively accurate portrayals of alcoholism and/or drug addiction on television and in the movies. However, behavioral addictions, also referred to as *process addictions*, are usually more difficult to fathom. Nevertheless, people can and do become addicted to highly pleasurable, self-soothing, dissociative *behaviors* just as often and just as easily as they become addicted to highly pleasurable, self-soothing, dissociative *substances*—and with similarly problematic results.

Can a Behavior Really Be Addictive?

The American Psychiatric Association is not overly accepting of behavioral addictions, excluding all but gambling addiction, from the latest edition of its *Diagnostic and Statistical Manual of Mental Disorders* (the DSM-5).[1] In fact, the APA has recently shied away from using the word addiction in general, now labeling alcoholism and drug addiction as "substance use disorders,"[2] and gambling addiction as "gambling disorder."[3] However, most other psychotherapeutic professional organizations are considerably more populist and forward-thinking, in particular the American Society of Addiction Medicine. In fact, ASAM's general definition of addiction, adopted in 2011, addresses behavioral addictions quite clearly, opening with the following language:

ADDICTION IS A PRIMARY, CHRONIC DISEASE of brain reward, motivation, memory and related circuitry. Dysfunction in these circuits leads to characteristic biological, psychological, social and spiritual manifestations. This is reflected in an individual pathologically pursuing reward and/or relief by substance use *and other behaviors* [emphasis added].[4]

Thanks in large part to the APA's behind-the-times stance, there is often a good deal of confusion among not only the general public but therapists too, when it comes to understanding, identifying, and treating behavioral addictions, including sexual addiction. However, this is largely unnecessary if/when one understands addiction's basic causes and origins.

In truth, addictions of all types form and manifest in the same basic ways. For starters, the risk factors for substance and behavioral addictions are the same—most often a combination of genetic and environmental factors.[5] In other words, people are at risk when there is a history of addiction (any type) or mental illness (any type) in the family, and/or they themselves have unresolved early-life or severe adult trauma. A lot of the time, these at-risk individuals turn to alcohol, prescription medications, or illicit substances as a way to self-medicate stress, emotional discomfort, and/or the pain of their underlying psychological conditions, but some will also turn to intensely pleasurable patterns of behavior to feel better.

Put very simply, addictive substances *and* addictive behaviors trigger the same basic neurochemical pleasure response—primarily the release of dopamine (pleasure), along with adrenaline (excitement), oxytocin (love and connection), serotonin (emotional well-being), and a variety of endorphins (euphoria)—resulting in feelings of pleasure, excitement, control, and, most important, distraction and emotional escape. Over time, some people learn that the easiest way to avoid feelings of stress and emotional discomfort is to ingest an addictive substance and/or to engage in a highly pleasurable (and therefore potentially addictive) behavior. Eventually these individuals begin to use these substances and/or behaviors not to feel better, *but to feel less* (i.e., to control what they feel). This is a sure sign of addiction. The only significant difference between substance and behavioral addictions is that substance addicts ingest alcohol or drugs to create an emotionally escapist neurochemical high, whereas behavioral addicts rely on an intensely pleasurable fantasy or activity to do the same thing, and some abuse both.

Part of the confusion around behavioral addictions arises because certain *potentially* addictive behaviors are (for most people, most of the time) healthy and essential to life. For instance, eating and being sexual contribute to survival of both the individual and the species. (This is why our brains are programmed to register/experience pleasure when we engage in these activities.) Unfortunately, for vulnerable people (people at risk for addiction thanks to genetics and/or their environment), this inborn pleasure response can become a go-to coping mechanism used to deal with any and all forms of emotional and/or psychological discomfort, turned to time and time again until the individual loses control over it.

To further understand the link between substance and behavioral addictions, consider a cocaine addict on payday. After receiving his check, he runs to the bank to exchange it for cash, perhaps skipping out of work early to do so. Then he dashes off to his dealer's house to spend money that he really ought to set aside for food, rent, childcare and the like. As he approaches his dealer's house, his heart races, he's sweating, and he is so obsessed and preoccupied with using that he doesn't even notice the police car parked a block away. He is so completely focused on cocaine that the day-to-day world, with all of its problems and obligations, has temporarily receded. In most respects *this individual is high already*. He has already escaped from his emotional life, his decision-making is distorted, and he has lost touch with healthy reality. It doesn't matter that there are no actual 'drugs' in his system because his brain is pumping out dopamine adrenaline and other pleasure/intensity-related neurochemicals leaving him feeling the same kind of high. Achieving and maintaining this neurobiological state of distraction and emotional escape, no matter how it is induced, is the goal for addicts.

Addiction is all about escaping emotional reality via the manipulation of our own neurochemistry, and this can happen with *or without* an addictive substance. Sex addicts in particular "get high" based more on fantasies and ritualistic preparations than anything else. In fact, sex addicts experience more pleasure and escape through anticipating, chasing, and preparing for sex than from the sex act itself. They even have a name for this condition, referring to it as *feeling like being in a bubble or a trance*. In other words, sex addiction is not so much about the sex act itself, rather it's about losing touch with emotional and sometimes realities for an extended period of time. For sex addicts, engaging in actual sex and reaching orgasm *ends the high* by throwing them back into the real world, where they must once again face life and all its problems, the very things they were trying to avoid and escape in the first place.

Common Behavioral (or Process) Addictions

Sex is not the only behavioral addiction. Others include:

- ✓ **Gambling:** Gambling addiction, also called gambling disorder and compulsive gambling, is an uncontrollable urge to gamble. Typically, gambling addicts will play whatever game is available, though their preference is fast-paced games like video poker, slots, blackjack, and roulette, where rounds end quickly and there is an immediate opportunity to play again. Digital technology now offers these games in abundance.
- ✓ **Love:** Love addiction is the compulsive search for romantic attachment. (This disorder is discussed in detail in Chapter 7.) Love addicts sacrifice time, health, money, self-esteem, and more in their pursuit of the perfect partner/love object.
- ✓ **Social Media:** Social media obsession is the quest to have the most friends or followers on sites/apps like Facebook, Twitter, and Instagram; to have one's lovingly constructed posts and tweets responded to in positive ways; and to "look good" through an endless series of (often) narcissistic posts. Social media addicts sometimes choose to bypass real world relationships, recreation, and social engagement for their online life.

✓ **Spending:** Spending addiction, also called *oniomania*, compulsive spending, shopping addiction, and compulsive buying disorder, occurs when people spend obsessively despite the damage this does to their finances and their relationships. The Internet has greatly escalated this problem as shopping is today a 24/7 possibility.

✓ **Video Gaming:** Video game addiction is the extreme use of computer and video games. Typically, gaming addicts play for at least two hours daily; some play four or five times that amount. They often neglect sleep, personal hygiene, diet, relationships, jobs, financial obligations, exercise, and life in general to be in the game.

Compulsions Versus Addictions

It may seem from the above discussion that almost anything can be addictive—substances and behaviors alike. This is not in fact the case. *For a substance or a behavior to be addictive, it needs to trigger the experience of pleasure* (the neurochemical pleasure response discussed above) *and cause anticipatory fantasy* (as with the cocaine user described above). Without these elements, a behavior may be compulsive, but it does not qualify as an addiction. For instance, compulsive hand-washing, (also produces a temporary feeling of emotional control and relief), though out of control and possibly causing negative consequences, evokes neither pleasure nor anticipatory fantasy. As such, it is not considered to be an addiction. Instead, this behavior is classified as an Obsessive-Compulsive Disorder (OCD).[6] In short, it is the endless, fantasy-driven anticipation of pleasure that drives addiction. Pleasure is the "carrot on a stick" that keeps an addict trudging forward.

Behavioral Addictions Can Be Tricky to Identify

Even though behavioral addictions are in most respects similar to substance addictions, they are often more difficult to identify. After all, they're easier to hide, they're (usually) more socially acceptable, and outside observers (even therapists) don't always recognize the behaviors as potentially addictive. As such, behavioral addicts will typically experience serious directly related consequences before being found out, confronted and/or seeking help. Sometimes behavioral addictions are only uncovered during treatment for a substance use disorder or some other psychiatric condition. For instance, a woman in treatment for depression and alcohol abuse may find herself flirting or acting out sexually with other patients or even staff, leading to an evaluation for sex and love addiction, or a man attending Alcoholics Anonymous may find himself continually relapsing at the local casino, leading to a realization that he has an intertwined alcohol and gambling addiction.

Another major obstacle in the identification and treatment of behavioral addictions is the fact that most people view them as being less serious than "real" addictions (i.e., substance addictions). In fact, nothing could be further from the truth. Behavioral addictions create the same types and degree of havoc as substance use disorders: relationship trouble, issues at work or in school, declining physical and/or emotional health (depression, anxiety, loss of self-esteem, etc.), isolation, financial woes, loss of interest in previously enjoyable activities, legal trouble, and worse; addiction *is* addiction.

Sexually Speaking:
A Basic Understanding of Sex Addiction

Sexual addiction, also called *hypersexuality*, *hypersexual disorder*, and *sexual compulsivity*, is a behavioral addiction focused on sex and sexual fantasy. More specifically, sex addiction is a dysfunctional pre-occupation with sexual urges, fantasies, and behaviors, often involving the obsessive pursuit of objectified non-intimate sexuality: pornography, casual/anonymous sex, prostitution, etc. This adult pattern of sexual urges, fantasies, and behaviors must continue for a period of at least six months, despite both related negative life consequences and (failed) attempts to either stop or curtail the pleasurable, but problem-inducing behaviors. In short, sex addiction is an ongoing, out-of-control pattern of compulsive sexual fantasies and behaviors that causes problems in the addict's life.

The consequences of sexual addiction can be quite varied in nature. For instance, a recent United Kingdom survey of 350 self-identified sex addicts found that sex addicts commonly experience the following problems:

Shame	70.5%
Low Self-Esteem	65.0%
Mental Health Issues	49.8%
Loss of a Relationship	46.5%
Sexual Dysfunction	26.7%
Serious Suicidality	19.4%
Sexually Transmitted Disease	19.4%
Other (Non-STD) Physical Health Problems	15.7%
Debt	14.7%
Impaired Parenting	14.7%
Legal Actions Against	06.0%
Loss of Employment	04.1%
Press Exposure	00.9%[7]

Like other addicts, sex addicts typically abuse both fantasy and behavior as ways to "numb out" and escape from stress and emotional (and sometimes physical) discomfort—including the pain of underlying emotional and/or psychological issues like depression, anxiety, early-life trauma abandonment fears and the like. In other words, sex addicts don't use compulsive sexual fantasies and behaviors to feel better, they use them to distract themselves from what they are feeling in that moment. As such, sexual addiction is not about having fun, no matter how good the sex itself, it's about controlling (by escaping) what one feels.

In sum, sex addicts are hooked on the dissociative euphoria produced by intense sexual fantasies and directly related patterns of sexual behavior (including their "endless" search for sex). They typically find as much excitement and escape in fantasizing about and searching for their next sexual encounter as in the sex act itself. Thus they can spend hours, sometimes even days, in this elevated emotional state—high on the goal/idea of having sex—before actually engaging in any concrete sexual act. Because of this, sex addicts spend much more time engaged in the fantasy and ritualized pursuit of sex than in the sex act itself.

Patterns of problematic fantasy-driven behavior typically exhibited by sex addicts often includes:

- ✓ Compulsive use of pornography, with or without masturbation
- ✓ Compulsive use of one or more digital "sexnologies," i.e., webcams, sexting, dating/hookup websites and hook-up apps, virtual reality sex games, sexual devices, etc.
- ✓ Consistently being "on the hunt" for sexual activity
- ✓ Multiple affairs or brief "serial" relationships
- ✓ Consistent involvement with strip clubs, adult bookstores, adult movie theaters, sex clubs, and other sex-focused environments

✓ Ongoing involvement with prostitution and/or sensual massage (hiring or providing)

✓ A pattern of anonymous and/or casual sexual hookups with people met online via apps, websites or in person

✓ Repeatedly engaging in unprotected sex

✓ Repeatedly engaging in sex with potentially dangerous people or in potentially dangerous places

✓ Seeking sexual experiences without regard to immediate or long-term potential consequences

✓ In some, repeated patterns of minor sexual offenses such as voyeurism, exhibitionism, frotteurism, etc.

Common Signs and Symptoms of Sexual Addiction

For the most part, the core signs and symptoms of sexual addiction are the same regardless of age, race, gender, social history, and psychological underpinnings. In fact, nearly all sex addicts report, in some form, the following:

✓ **Obsessive Sexual Fantasy and Preoccupation:** Sex addicts obsess about romance and sex. They spend hours, sometimes even days, fantasizing about it, planning for it, pursuing it, and engaging in it. The majority of their decisions revolve around sex, including what they wear, which gym they go to, the car they drive, their relationships, and perhaps even the career path they choose.

✓ **Loss of Control:** Sex addicts lose control over their ability to choose to not engage in sexual fantasies and behaviors. They try to quit or cut back, making promises to themselves and/or others, but they repeatedly fail in these efforts.

✓ **Related Adverse Consequences:** Sex addicts eventually experience the same basic negative life consequences that alcoholics, drug addicts, compulsive gamblers, compulsive spenders, and all other addicts deal with, such as job loss, trouble in school, financial woes, ruined relationships, declining physical and/or emotional health, loss of interest in previously enjoyable activities, loss of time, isolation, arrest, etc.

✓ **Tolerance and Escalation:** With substance addiction, tolerance and escalation manifest when the addict must take more of a substance or a stronger substance to achieve and maintain the same high that he or she seeks. With sexual addiction, tolerance and escalation occur when the addict spends increasing amounts of time engaging in the addiction, or when the intensity level of his/her sexual fantasies and activities increases. Over time, thanks to tolerance and escalation, many sex addicts find themselves engaging in sexual behaviors that hadn't even occurred to them early in the addictive process. Some act out in ways that violate their personal moral code, their spiritual beliefs, and perhaps even the law. Some escalate to viewing illicit or bizarre images, and others simply lose increasing amounts of valuable time and energy to sex.

✓ **Withdrawal:** With sexual addiction, withdrawal tends to manifest not so much physically, as often occurs with substance abuse (i.e., delirium tremens when detoxing from alcohol), but emotionally and psychologically. Sex addicts in withdrawal tend to become either depressive or restless, lonely, irritable, and discontented. As with tolerance, withdrawal is not a necessary element of the sex addiction diagnosis, but most sex addicts do experience the feeling of it.

✓ **Denial:** Denial keeps sex addicts out of touch with the process, costs, and reality of their addiction. They routinely ignore the kinds of warning signs that would be obvious to a healthier person. Often, they externalize blame onto people or situations for the consequences of their sexual acting out. In short, they are often unable or unwilling to see the destructive effects wrought by their sexual behavior until a related crisis shows up at the door.

Another way to look at the signs and symptoms of sexual addiction is with the "SAFE" formula developed by Dr. Patrick Carnes, a pioneer in the diagnosis and treatment of sexual addiction. Dr. Carnes uses SAFE as an acronym for Secret, Abusive, Feelings, and Empty. In his book, *Out of the Shadows*, he writes:

THE QUESTION EMERGES FOR ADDICTS as to how they determine when their sexual behavior is addictive. The following formula is suggested as a guideline. Signs of compulsive sexuality are when the behavior can be described as follows:

1) **It is a secret.** Anything that cannot pass public scrutiny will create the shame of a double life.

2) **It is abusive to self or others.** Anything that is exploitive or harmful to others or degrades oneself will activate the addictive system.

3) **It is used to avoid or is a source of painful feelings.** If sexuality is used to alter moods or results in painful mood shifts, it is clearly part of the addictive process.

4) **It is empty of a caring, committed relationship.** Fundamental to the whole concept of addiction and recovery is the healthy dimension of human relationships.[8]

Throughout the 20th century sex addiction specialists tended to place a considerable amount of emphasis on committed, monogamous relationships (see the "empty" portion of the Carnes SAFE formula) as the endpoint of recovery from sexual addiction. Over time, however, we have learned that marriage and long-term commitments are not an absolute requirement for everyone wishing to achieve sexual healing and/or sexual sobriety (unless one is already in a committed, long-term monogamous relationship). In today's world, healing from sexual addiction can encompass many types of meaningful, open and honest sexual or romantic connections—as long as they are not secretive, abusive to self or others, repeatedly used to avoid feelings, or causing problems to the addict and/or the addict's loved ones.

In short, sex addicts needn't be married to be in sexual recovery. But they do need to be connected to their sexual partners and not treat or use them as objects. In fact, there are individuals in sexual recovery who have experienced such significant early-life trauma that they might never be able to create and sustain meaningful monogamy. But that does not mean they can't heal, be in recovery, develop meaningful interpersonal connections (sexual and otherwise), and feel happy and at peace with themselves. In other words, today we see that sexual recovery is less about cultural norms and more about personal integrity relationship building that may or may not involve sex, and the elimination of impulsive and problematic sexual behavior.

The Cycle of Sexual Addiction

All addictions are cyclical in nature, with no clear beginning or end and one stage leading to the next (and then the next, and the next, and the next), leaving the addict stuck in an endless, downwardly spiraling loop. With sexual addiction, various models of the addictive cycle have been proposed, modified, and expanded upon, and there are now many versions, each with merit.[9] I generally prefer and utilize a six-stage model that follows.

The Cycle of Sexual Addiction[10]

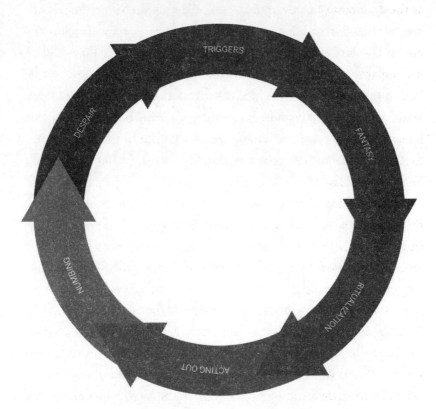

Stage One–Triggers (Shame/Blame/Guilt/Other Strong Emotions): Triggers are catalysts that create a need/desire to act out sexually. Most often triggers are some sort of "pain agent." Pain agents include both emotional/psychological and physical discomfort, either short-term or long-term. Depression, anxiety, loneliness, boredom, stress, shame, anger, and any other uncomfortable feeling can easily trigger a sex addict's desire to escape, avoid, and dissociate. Positive agents can also serve as triggers like the icing on a cake. So if a sex addict gets fired from his or her job, he or she will want to act out sexually; and if that same addict gets a great new job, he or she will want act out sexually. Triggers can also be visual (seeing a sexy image on a billboard), auditory (hearing a noise that reminds the addict of sexual activity), olfactory (smelling the perfume of a past sexual partner), or even touch or taste related. If such triggers are not recognized early and dealt with in a healthy way (dissipated via a healthy, nonaddictive coping mechanism like talking to supportive friends, family members, or a therapist), then the cycle inevitably slides forward into stage two.

Stage Two–Fantasy: After being triggered and therefore needing to emotionally escape and dissociate, sex addicts often unconsciously turn to their primary coping mechanism: sexual fantasy. They start thinking about how much they enjoyed past sexual encounters and how much they would enjoy a sexual encounter either right now or in the near future. At this point, the addict is preoccupied to the point of obsession with his or her sexual fantasies. On this day they might flirt with the grocery clerk that they barely noticed just a day or two prior. Every person encountered by the addict (both in person and online) is viewed as a sexual object or simply "in the way." The addict's fantasies do not involve memories of prior bad experiences or related negative consequences. Once the addict's mind is mired in fantasy, it is very difficult to stop the addictive cycle without some sort of outside intervention.

Stage Three–Ritualization: Ritualization is where fantasy moves toward reality. This stage adds excitement, intensity, and arousal. For example, the addict logs on to the computer and goes to his or her favorite porn site, or hops in the car and drives to a place where sex workers congregate, or begins the process of booking an out-of-town business trip on which he or she can act out sexually without restraint, or simply opens up their favorite "adult friend finder" app. This stage of the cycle is also known as *the bubble* or *the trance* because the addict is psychologically and emotionally lost to it. Real-world concerns disappear as the addict focuses more and more intently on his or her sexual fantasies. This stage of the addiction (rather than the sex act itself) evokes the escapist neurochemical high that (sex) addicts seek. As such, sex addicts typically try to stretch this stage out for as long as possible—looking at porn, cruising for casual sex, chatting via webcams, losing hours on a sex app, and the like for many hours (or even days) before moving to the next stage.

Stage Four–Sexual Acting Out: Most non-sex addicts think that this stage, is the ultimate goal of sexual addiction, because this is where actual sex and orgasm takes place (either solo or with others). However, as stated above, the fantasy-fueled escape and dissociation of this stage is the real objective. In fact, many will try to put off actual sex and orgasm for as long as possible because *orgasm ends the fantasy driven escapist high* and tosses the addict back into the real world with all of its issues and problems. In other words, sex addicts are seeking more to escape emotional discomfort, than to experience the pleasure of orgasm. Orgasm brings their high to an abrupt, screeching halt.

Stage Five–Numbing: After acting out, sex addicts attempt to emotionally distance themselves emotionally from what they've just done. They justify their behaviors, telling themselves, *If my spouse was nicer to me, I wouldn't need to do this.* They minimize their behaviors, telling themselves, *Nobody knows that I just spent six hours looking at and masturbating to pornography, and nobody got hurt by what I did, so it's no big deal.* They rationalize their behaviors, telling themselves, *Hooking up with people online for mutual masturbation isn't really cheating because I don't actually* *touch the other person and I don't even give that person my real name,* etc. In other words, in this stage of the cycle the addict's denial kicks in full force as a way to temporarily protect him or her from the next stage.

Stage Six–Despair (Shame/Anxiety/Depression): Eventually, numbing will dissipate for most sex addicts. And when it does, many will start to feel ashamed and remorseful. Exacerbating these unwanted emotions is the fact that they also feel powerless to stop the cycle of their addiction. Plus, whatever reality it was that they were trying to escape in the first place returns, bringing with it whatever self-loathing, anxiety, and depression they were already experiencing. And, as you may recall, this is exactly the sort of emotional discomfort that triggers sexual addiction in the first place. As such, over time, stage six spins the self-perpetuating cycle right back to stage one. Where it starts all over again.

Repeating the Cycle Builds Tolerance AND Trains the Brain

The sexual addiction cycle typically intensifies with each repetition, requiring more of the same behavior or more intense behavior to reach or maintain the same neurochemical high over time. This transforms from a repetitive loop into a downward spiral— one characteristic of all forms of addiction—leading to relationship, work, health, financial, legal, and other crises. And all of these crises also qualify as emotional triggers, which can set the same process in motion yet again.

How Can the Cycle Be Stopped?

The cycle of sexual addiction is best interrupted in the early portion of stage one, when the addict's emotional triggers (the experiences and emotions that activate a desire to sexually act out) first arise. If and when the addict learns to recognize the early signs of emotional discomfort like stress, certain types of imagery, people, situations, places, then he or she can engage in contrary actions designed to:

A: Stop the escalating fantasies before they lead into ritualization and acting out

B: Deal with the unwanted uncomfortable feelings or triggers in an emotionally healthy way and not act them out

This will be discussed in greater detail in later chapters.

One Man's Story:
Sexual Addiction Is NOT...

AT THE AGE OF TWENTY, STEVEN CAME OUT AS GAY to his highly religious parents. Members of a very conservative sect, they struggled to accept his "choice" as normal and decided to seek advice from their pastor. Based on *his belief system*, their pastor—a trained and licensed pastoral counselor—told them that Steven was likely suffering from sexual addiction, suggesting intensive sexual addiction treatment with another religiously-based therapist. In this treatment, Steven was given a variety of highly homophobic tasks to complete (participating in contact sports, which he hated, mimicking the way that heterosexual men walk and talk, which felt unnatural to him, becoming more assertive with women through flirting, which caused distress to not only him but his female friends who knew he was gay, etc.) Needless to say, this well-meaning but homophobic therapist's attempts to change Steven's "sexually addictive behavior" failed miserably. And, sadly, this failure disheartened Steven, who over time turned to alcohol and later methamphetamine as a way to numb his increasing levels of emotional discomfort. Though he was not then nor did he ever become sexually addicted, he did struggle with substance abuse, eventually entering treatment at a non-religious facility, where they helped him address not only his substance use disorder but also his shame about being homosexual. Today he is a sober gay man with a husband and a much-loved six-year-old son.

Unfortunately, some people may misuse the label "sex addiction" to define virtually any type of sexual behavior that doesn't meet their own moral standards (religious, cultural, personal, etc.).

- ✓ She's had two affairs, so she must be a sex addict.
- ✓ He's been having sex with men. Obviously, he's a sex addict.
- ✓ In our church you can be excommunicated for looking at porn. I hear that he looked at porn at least half a dozen times, so he must be a sex addict. Why else would he take risks like that?

Other individuals can misuse the sex addiction label as a catchall excuse for virtually any type of sexual misconduct. In other words, people who get caught red-handed engaging in inappropriate, problematic, possibly even illegal sexual behavior will sometimes blame their actions on an addiction, hoping to avoid or at least to minimize the judgment and/or punishment they experience. Occasionally these individuals really are sexually addicted, but just as often they are not. Either way, *a diagnosis of sexual addiction is never intended to justify bad behavior, or to let people off the hook for what they've done.*

Unfortunately, it's not just layperson or media-generated "diagnoses" that cause problems. Plenty of well-meaning but under-informed therapists are willing to label all sorts of things as sexual addiction, as happened with Steven (above). To a large extent this is because, surprisingly, the mental health profession in the U.S. provides minimal required training in human sexual behavior. Because of this, some therapists mistakenly believe that any form of sexual or gender-driven *dysphoria* (unhappiness, shame, and self-loathing) should be treated as an addiction. This is simply not the case. The fact that an individual feels bad about his or her sexualized thoughts, feelings, desires, or actions does not mean that he or she is a sex addict for engaging in them. Yes, that individual *might* be a sex addict, but only if his or her behavior meets the primary criteria for a sexual addiction diagnosis: ongoing obsession, loss of control, and repeated negative consequences and all the rest.

For clarity, below I have compiled a list of things that sex addiction is *not*.

- ✓ **Sex addiction is not fun.** When you say the words sexual addiction, the knee-jerk response is often something like: "Hey, sounds fun. Sign me up." In truth, sex addiction is the opposite of fun. It is a compulsion that leads to shame, depression, anxiety, and a wide variety of negative consequences, just like every other form of addiction. Sex addiction is not about having a good time any more than alcoholism is about having a good time.

- ✓ **Sex addiction is not an excuse for bad behavior.** As mentioned above, many of the people who get caught engaging in some embarrassing, objectionable (like an affair), or illegal sexual behavior try to use sex addiction as a catchall excuse, hoping to avoid or at least to minimize the judgment and/or punishment they might experience. Sometimes these individuals really are sexually addicted, but just as often they are not. Either way, a diagnosis of sexual addiction never *justifies* bad behavior. Rather than providing an excuse, a diagnosis of sexual addiction provides an obligation to recognize the issue and to behave differently in the future. *Under no circumstances are sex addicts absolved of responsibility for the problems their choices have caused.* In fact, part of healing from sexual addiction is admitting what you've done, accepting any consequences, and making amends as best you can.

✓ **Sex addiction is not related to sexual orientation or gender identity.** Neither homosexual, bisexual nor trans related arousal patterns are factors in the diagnosis of sexual addiction, even if those arousal patterns are ego-*dystonic* (unwanted). Being gay, lesbian, bisexual or transgender does not make you a sex addict any more than being straight makes you a sex addict. Sometimes self-loathing homosexuals, transgender people, or bisexuals will seek out sex addiction treatment, hoping it will change their sexual orientation or identity. Occasionally they do this at the behest of a misguided clinician, as occurred with Steven in the example above. However, changing one's arousal template is not possible.[11] If you're attracted to men, that's the way it is; if you're attracted to women, same story; and if you like both genders, you'd better get used to it because that's not going change no matter how much analysis you have or how many twelve-step meetings you attend. Put simply, *sexual addiction is not in any way defined by who or what it is that turns you on.* (See chapter on Sexual Orientation for more information.)

✓ **Sex addiction is not related to fetishes or paraphilias (kink).** Fetishes and paraphilias are recurrent, intense, sexually arousing fantasies, urges and/or behaviors involving nonhuman objects, specific body parts, the suffering of oneself or one's sexual partner, or nonconsensual sex (in appearance or actuality). We're talking about BDSM (a la *Fifty Shades of Grey*), foot worship, chubby chasing, diapers/infantilism, etc. Fetishes and paraphilias may cause a person to keep sexual secrets, to feel shame and/or distress, and even to feel out of control, but they are not indicators of sexual addiction. In fact, they are pathologized only if they cause significant distress and/or impairment of social, occupational, or other important areas of functioning to that individual.[12] And even when a fetish or paraphilia does qualify as pathologic (example: bestiality), it is still not the same thing as sexual addiction. So, once again, sexual addiction is not in any way defined by who or what it is that turns you on. Many people have sexual concerns but are not sex addicts.

✓ **Sex addiction is not just a guy thing.** The common perception is that only men are sex addicts. This is not true. Plenty of women are sexually and romantically addicted. That said, men are usually easier to diagnose, because they are generally more forthcoming about the purely sexual nature of what they are doing. Women, on the other hand, tend to talk about sex in terms of relationships, even when they're having just as much sex, and the same types of sex, as their male counterparts. More about women in later chapters.

✓ **Sex addiction is not driven by drug use.** Sometimes drug users and drug addicts, particularly those who abuse cocaine, methamphetamine, and other stimulant/party drugs, can become hypersexual when high. This can occur especially in men when they add Viagra or another erection-enhancing drug to the mix. This does not, however, make these people sex addicts. If the hypersexual behavior ends when the drug use ends, then a diagnosis of sexual addiction is not likely appropriate.

✓ **Sexual addiction is not a symptom of bipolar disorder, ADHD (attention-deficit/hyperactivity disorder), OCD (obsessive-compulsive disorder), or any other psychiatric condition.** In order for the diagnosis of sexual addiction to be made, professionals must first rule out any number of major mental health disorders that sometimes include hypersexuality or impulsive sexual behavior as a possible symptom. Some of these include the active stages of bipolar disorder, obsessive-compulsive disorder, and attention-deficit/hyperactivity disorder.[13] In other words, not everyone who is impulsively or compulsively sexual has a problem driven by sexual addiction; hypersexual and impulsive sexual behaviors are legitimate symptoms of many other disorders. That said, it is certainly possible to have any of the aforementioned psychiatric conditions and also be sexually addicted. Much as an alcoholic can also have OCD, etc.

✓ **Sex addiction is not the same thing as sexual offending.** By definition, sexual offending involves either illegal and/or nonconsensual sexual behavior. This is not the same thing as sexual addiction. Yes, the behavior of approximately 10 percent of all sex addicts may escalate into offending—most often engaging in lower-level offenses like voyeurism, exhibitionism, viewing inappropriate pornography, and engaging in prostitution. Nevertheless, *sexual offending is not indicative of sexual addiction.* It is critically important that the criteria for sex addiction be very strictly applied when dealing with sex offenders, as these individuals are the group most likely to self-identify as sex addicts in an attempt to avoid judgment and/or punishment.

✓ **Sex addiction therapy is sex positive!** In some quarters, there is a fear that sex addiction therapists are trying to be the new "sex police," imposing moral, cultural, and/or religious values on sexuality, thereby creating a narrow version of sexual health. Sadly, as we saw in the example with Steven, this fear is not entirely unfounded. There are indeed some moralist and/or highly religiously driven therapists who misuse and misapply the sex addiction diagnosis, using it to marginalize and pathologize sexual behaviors that don't mesh with their personal or religious belief systems. Homosexuality, bisexuality, transgenderism, recreational porn use, casual sex, polyamory, and fetishes—all of which today fall within the spectrum of normal and healthy adult sexuality—have at times been misdiagnosed as sexual addiction.

In reality, as stated previously, *sexual addiction has nothing whatsoever to do with who or what it is that turns a person on*. Instead, as described throughout this book, sex addiction is about using the excitement and intensity of sexual fantasies and behaviors (of whatever kind) to emotionally numb out by evoking emotional arousal, excitement and fantasy-fueled distraction.

Am I Addicted to Sex?

MICHAEL IS A MARRIED, TWENTY-NINE-YEAR-OLD professional property manager who grew up in an alcoholic and occasionally abusive household. He started looking at porn at age twelve, usually for a few minutes at a time (staying online for as long as it took to "get off"). Over time, his sexual forays escalated in both time and intensity. By the end of high school, he had also begun sneaking off to the "bad parts of town" to visit prostitutes on weekends. After high-school graduation, he took a job with a local real estate manager and started dating the sister of a coworker. Because he really liked her, he stopped seeing prostitutes and simultaneously cut back on his porn usage. At the age of twenty-three, they were married, and "being in love" he quit porn altogether. Or so he thought. A year later, Michael's wife was six months pregnant when he suddenly "found himself" online, compulsively masturbating to pornography. Before the baby was born, he was back to seeing prostitutes. Now, at age twenty-nine, he spends nearly all of his free time either looking at porn or hooking up with women he meets on apps like Ashley Madison and Tinder. (Some of these women are prostitutes, some not.) He says that his wife does not know what he does with his time—she just thinks that he works very long hours—but he feels terrible about his behavior. He says that the extramarital sex is not fun and that he desperately wants to stop, but he can never seem to manage that for more than a few days at a time. He also longs to spend more time with his young kids, but more often than not chooses to sexually act out only to later hate himself for it.

Understanding the World of a Sex Addict

For active sex addicts, sexually addictive activity takes place regardless of outward success, intelligence, physical attractiveness, existing intimate relationships, or anything else. Very often sex addicts, feeling shameful or fearful, will tell themselves, "This is the last time that I am going to behave in this way," yet ultimately they are compelled to return to the same or a similar sexual situation, over and over again. Over time, they organize their lives around sexual fantasy and the behaviors that follow. They spend inordinate amounts of time thinking about, planning for, pursuing, and engaging in sexual activity (with themselves and/or others). Sex becomes an obsession to the point where important relationships (with spouses, kids, parents, friends, etc.), interests (exercise, hobbies, creativity, etc.), and responsibilities (work, finances, childcare, etc.) are ignored. Oftentimes sex addicts' behaviors escalate to the point where they violate their inner values and moral code, which both creates and intensifies their shame. And because they feel so much shame about what they are doing, they nearly always find themselves leading a double life, keeping their sexual acting out hidden and a secret from family, friends, and everyone else who matters to them.

Admittedly, every sex addict's story is different. Michael's, however, is relatively common in many respects. He started young, using porn and masturbation to feel better, not merely to explore his sexuality. Over time, his sexual behaviors escalated, and eventually he found himself looking at porn for hours on end and seeing prostitutes whenever he could afford it. Furthermore, his actions from the start were designed to escape the sad realities of his young life—in his case, the emotional discomfort of living in an alcoholic and abusive household. On top of that, he wants to quit and has tried to quit, but can't seem to manage it. Finally, and most tellingly, even though he has not yet been found out by his wife, he is nevertheless experiencing negative life consequences: primarily feelings of shame and remorse. This had led to his further emotionally distancing himself from his family leaving him even more isolated and depressed.

Another Man's Story:
Sexual Addiction Is . . .

JAMES IS A TWENTY-TWO-YEAR-OLD MAN who left school a few years back for a relationship that didn't work out. He is feeling depressed, as if his life is going nowhere, and so lately he has started seeing a therapist. In his first therapy session, James says that he started looking at online pornography when he was thirteen, and by the time he finished high school he was using porn daily, often for several hours at a time, despite several attempts to cut back. He says that over time he has lost interest in nearly all of the activities he once enjoyed—sports, school, video games, and just plain hanging out with his friends—preferring instead to view porn and have webcam sex with anyone who's willing. Once an excellent student, his grades dropped steadily throughout high school to the point where he was barely accepted into college. And he dropped out of college after his second semester because "dropping out" seemed like a better option than "failing out." Since then, he has held several menial jobs, none for more than a few months. He now lives with his parents. James has not had a girlfriend since his sophomore year of high school, even though he wants one. He tells his therapist that he views cybersex as a solution to his problems, as it "makes him feel better," not a potential cause. He says that he does not want to even discuss his sexual behavior, and that he only wants to treat his depression.

Defining Sexual Addiction

James appears to be a sad, isolated, and depressed young man whose single source of distraction and emotional excitement seems to be porn and nothing but porn. Despite his (understandable) insistence that sex is not part of his problem, it clearly is; in fact it is likely the primary source, if not primary symptom, of current problems and must be addressed early on. This is where skillful therapy with a well-trained sex addiction specialist could help him shift from "protecting his source/porn" (think of a heroin addict protecting his sources), to understanding the degree to which it is destroying his young life.

One—Preoccupation with Sexual Fantasy and Acting Out Those Fantasies to the Point of Obsession. Note how James' life focus in the story above reflects a repositioning of his priorities. He reports having lost interest over time in sports, video games, hanging out with friends, etc. And (even though not openly stated) that he is putting all that time now into porn. He is not looking for a romantic partner, job, recreation, or connection. His daily priority is to access and engage porn.

Two—Loss of Control Over Stopping or Changing Sexual Behavior. James reports having tried on several occasions to "cut back" or "alter" his porn use—especially when he was younger—but failed. Note that in his story (above) he doesn't even want to consider stopping at this point. By the time he gets to therapy, he sees the porn as the only thing that keeps him feeling good. While clearly depressed, he is likely afraid that he will only get more so—if he let's go of the porn. He is also (as are many sex addicts early to the healing process), likely afraid of trying again (to stop) and failing. So he has not given up—he has given into the porn. He has lost control over his abuse of it.

Three—Negative Life Consequences (indirectly or directly) Related to Sexual Fantasy and Behaviors. Clearly James is depressed and stuck. On an emotional level he is, essentially, the same mixed-up adolescent who started abusing porn compulsively nine years ago. He is isolated, with not much of a social life and few prospects for future education/work that interests him. He has no goals, few friends, has apparently withdrawn from life. Overall he is feeling pretty hopeless—which, while an obvious symptom of depression—and he may well be depressed—he nonetheless has the energy and focus to lose himself to cybersex day after day—hour after hour—which is so out of balance with the rest of his life—no wonder he is depressed!

Am I Sexually Addicted?

Sexual addiction can be difficult to recognize, especially for those who are mired in it. Because of its highly secretive nature, sex addiction can also be difficult for outside observers (family members, friends, employers, and even therapists) to identify and diagnose. There are, however, tools designed to help determine who is sexually addicted and who is not. Before looking at these tools in depth, it is useful to understand the primary differences between casual, at-risk and addicted users of highly objectified, non-intimate sexuality.

✓ **Casual users** are men and women who find non-intimate sexuality (online pornography, virtual sex, digital flirting, casual/ anonymous hookups, affairs, and the like) to be fascinating or fun. They get involved in these pleasurable distractions occasionally. Much of the time their behavior is driven either by curiosity and novelty, or life-stage events like a divorce. For instance, they may engage in non-intimate sexual activities (online or real world) more in late adolescence or after a relationship breakup. Typically, casual users of sexual fantasy and activity find non-intimate sex to be an intermittent source of relaxation and fun, but ultimately not as meaningful and satisfying as deeper, more intimate connections. As such, their interest in non-intimate sex is not often sustained over time.

✓ **At-risk users** are men and women who go through periods of intense objectified non-intimate sexuality, more often than not using it as a distraction from emotional discomfort and other life issues. They may have addiction-like periods, but they can (and usually do) limit or stop their behaviors if/when they start to experience (or even to see the possibility of experiencing) adverse consequences. Sometimes at-risk users may look a lot like addicted users, hiding the nature and extent of their sexual behaviors, temporarily ignoring potential and even actual consequences, even escalating the nature and extent of their use. What differentiates at-risk users from addicted users is this. At-risk users can stop on their own while addicted users cannot. In other words, at-risk users retain control and choice over their engagement with sexual fantasy and activity. Addicted users do not.

✓ **Addicted users** are men and women who compulsively and repeatedly use objectified non-intimate sexual images and experiences as a means of emotional escape and dissociation, regardless of potential and/or actual consequences to themselves or others. In other words, addicted users repetitively use sexual fantasy and activity as a way to numb out, not feel stress, and other forms of emotional discomfort. Typically, they lead a double life, separating their charged sexual activity from their work and home life: keeping secrets, telling lies, manipulating, juggling, minimizing, justifying, etc. When active in their addiction they can lack empathy for those negatively affected by their addiction, including spouses and partners, kids, friends, neighbors, and employers. Sometimes they even blame their "need to escape" on the attitudes and actions of these other people.

Here are ten key signs of sexual addiction.[1]

1) A pattern of out-of-control sexual behavior
2) Severe or ongoing life consequences due to sexual behavior
3) An inability to stop sexual behavior despite adverse consequences and previous attempts to stop
4) Persistent pursuit of self-destructive or high-risk sexual behavior (to self or others)
5) Important social, recreational, or occupational activities are sacrificed or reduced because of sexual behavior
6) Ongoing desire for change or failed attempts to limit sexual behavior
7) Sexual obsession and fantasy are becoming primary emotional coping strategies

8) The amount of time spent in sexual activity or the intensity of sexual experiences increases because the current level is insufficient

9) Severe mood changes around sexual activity (before, during, or after)

10) Inordinate amounts of time spent in obtaining sex, being sexual, or recovering from sexual experiences

It is not necessary that all ten signs be present for a self-diagnosis of sexual addiction; as few as two or three may indicate the onset of a serious problem. That said, with sexual addiction, most if not all of the signs are usually present to some extent, and those that are not yet present are typically looming on the near horizon.

A more detailed evaluation is available online to help you if you have more questions. You can access it at *hcibooks.com*.

Sex Addiction— the Basics: Triggers, Escalation, and Denial

Regardless of the addiction, be it substance or behavioral, there are three underlying components that most often drive and perpetuate the problem: triggers, escalation, and denial. As you may recall, triggers and escalation were discussed briefly in Chapter 1. Because they are so important and so pervasive in all forms of addiction, including sexual addiction, those two topics are addressed more fully in this chapter, along with addiction's third underlying element, denial. Before addressing these three topics, however, it is useful to have a solid understanding of what addiction does to the human brain.

The Neurobiology of Addiction

One of the questions most commonly asked by sex addicts and their loved ones is: why is it so hard to just stop? To answer this question, it helps to understand the ways in which addiction affects the human brain.

Essentially, in a normal, healthy (non-addicted) brain our naturally occuring "pleasure" or "rewards center"—registers pleasurable feelings in response to naturally occurring, life-affirming behaviors such as eating, helping others, joining with our community, being sexual, etc. These activities are rewarded because they (feel good) also ensure survival of both the individual and the human species. This is intelligent design (or evolution) at its finest. These sensations of pleasure result from the release of various neurochemicals, primarily dopamine, along with adrenaline, serotonin, oxytocin, and a few others.

When pleasure is experienced in the brain's rewards center, other portions of the brain are alerted, most notably those involving mood, memory, and decision-making. Basically, the rewards center tells the mood, memory, and decision-making regions how much it enjoyed eating, helping, or having sex etc. In this way we learn which activities are pleasurable. Over time, we associate these behaviors with enjoyment and a sense of well-being, and we make future decisions based on this information.

Unfortunately, our rewards center can also be manipulated. For instance, alcohol, addictive drugs, and compulsive patterns of intensely stimulating behaviors (sex, romance, gambling, spending, video gaming, etc.) can be abused to artificially stimulate the system, flooding the brain with unusually high levels of dopamine—anywhere from two to hundreds of times the amount provided by normal pleasurable activity. That's a pretty big blast of pleasure juice! And, as is the case with other pleasurable experiences, this enjoyment-related information is transmitted to areas of the brain dealing with mood, memory, and decision-making.[1] So is it any wonder that we sometimes want more, more, and still more things that feel, taste, sound, smell so good? (Think sex, chocolate, winning, approval, etc.)

Making matters worse, our brains are built to adapt to the input received. Over time, as addictive inputs are continually being engaged (through repetitive drug use, gambling, sex, or whatever), the brain adjusts to excessive dopamine levels by producing less and less dopamine and/or eliminating dopamine receptors.[2] (Dopamine is experienced as pleasure when it "plugs in" to a dopamine receptor.) In other words, as addiction sets in, the brain becomes conditioned to *expect* artificially high amounts of dopamine (pleasure).[3] In this way, *liking* an addictive substance or behavior can transform into *wanting/needing* an addictive substance or behavior, and then compulsion takes over meaning *having to have* it. So even though the addictive stimulus (drugs, alcohol, sex, romance, gambling, etc.) no longer provides the level of pleasure it once did, addicts *want/need* to continue using.

This is where triggers, escalation, and denial come into play.

Understanding Triggers

EDWIN IS A FORTY-SEVEN-YEAR-OLD SALESMAN for a hardwood flooring manufacturer. He has been in recovery for both sex and drug addiction for more than a year—entering therapy after his wife found out that he'd been cheating on her with several female clients, as well as going to strip clubs and prostitutes, while frequently drinking and doing cocaine at the same time. Though he lives in the suburbs, his office is located in the industrial section of town, and any even remotely convenient route to and from work takes him directly past at least one or two strip clubs and numerous street corners frequented by drug dealers and prostitutes. Most days Edwin does not even think about the strip clubs, drug dealers, or prostitutes when he's driving past them. But lately he is becoming increasingly aware that when he and his wife have been arguing, when he's had a hard day at work, when he's feeling frustrated, tired or stressed out, he simply can't seem to stop thinking about these women. On two different occasions he has "slipped" on his way home from work, once "finding himself" drunk and high in a strip club, another time "ending up" in the backseat of his car with a prostitute. And he can't understand why he has these moments of weakness when he's working so hard to heal from his addiction.

Triggers are the thoughts, experiences and feelings that induce the strong desire—the *craving*—to ingest an addictive substance or engage in an addictive behavior. When addictive cravings set in, it is very difficult to stop the ensuing addiction cycle.[4] This is why addicts sometimes find it so hard to remain sober, despite their best efforts.

A few of Edwin's triggers above include fighting with his wife, driving through the dicey neighborhood near his workplace, and feeling left out or pushed aside for any reason. As is the case for most addicts, when Edwin is feeling triggered, these powerful cravings begin. Thus, he becomes less and less able to control his sexual desires and fantasies. This is most apparent in the language he uses to describe his slips: "finding himself" in a strip club, and "ending up" in his car with a prostitute. That is very different than "deciding" or "choosing" to do something. And yet, that is exactly how he feels when triggered—as if he is "out of control" and literally feeling "pulled" toward his object of sexual fantasy and emotional escape.

Addiction cravings are not the same as a non-addicted person craving a bag of potato chips or a scoop of ice cream. Addictive cravings are more like the need for air after holding your breath for a minute or more. Once triggered, addictive cravings begin to overwhelm our conscious control, escaping all reason and logic (as does much emotionally driven, impulsive behavior). They are so powerful that they simply overwhelm and take control of an addict's thought process. As such, incredibly smart people can make really dumb decisions about the use and abuse of an addictive substance or behavior.

Unfortunately, anything that triggers the brain to remember the long-lost pleasure of addiction is a potential precursor for cravings and relapse.

Internal triggers typically involve emotional (or sometimes physical discomfort) of any kind—depression, shame, anxiety, anger, fear, guilt, remorse, boredom, etc. For instance, if/when a married sex addict's spouse is away for a few days (or even a few hours), he or she might feel lonely, and this emotional discomfort might trigger a desire to act out sexually.

External triggers can be people, places, things, and/or events. For instance, if/when a sex addict sees an old partner he/she used to have sex with, he or she might be triggered to act out sexually.

Addicts must also deal with intertwined triggers (both external and internal). For instance, if/when a sex addict argues with his or her spouse or has a bad day at work (an external trigger), he or she is likely to experience emotional discomfort say frustration or anger (internal triggers), with both triggers leading to a desire to sexually act out. And this desire may be exacerbated by visual triggers that remind the addict of his or her addiction (such as driving past strip clubs, prostitutes, and drug dealers).

Interestingly, not all triggers are negative. Sometimes material successes and positive emotions will evoke a desire to celebrate, and thus a desire to drink, use drugs, act out sexually, gamble, spend, etc.

A few of the more common *internal* triggers for sexual acting-out are:

- ✓ Any unmet need for validation and/or affection
- ✓ Unresolved resentments and anger
- ✓ Loneliness
- ✓ Boredom

✓ Fear
✓ Anxiety
✓ Frustration
✓ Low self-esteem
✓ Shame (feeling useless, worthless, and/or unlovable)
✓ Stress
✓ Feeling unappreciated
✓ Sadness or grief

A few of the more common *external* triggers for sexual acting-out are:

✓ Unstructured time alone
✓ Travel (especially alone)
✓ Relationship breakups, changes, and losses
✓ Unexpected life changes (job, finances, etc.)
✓ Unexpected losses or tragedies
✓ Highly stimulating positive experiences (having a baby, getting promoted)
✓ Drug and/or alcohol use
✓ Unexpected exposure to sexual stimuli (i.e., a Victoria's Secret catalog, a sexy billboard, driving by a strip club, seeing a prostitute, encountering an attractive person, etc.)
✓ Arguments
✓ Reprimands
✓ Financial insecurity
✓ Trouble within the family (like a child struggling at school)
✓ An emotionally or physically unavailable spouse

Both of the above lists could be extended ad infinitum, as each person's triggers are individual to them. Even memories of past traumas can be present-day triggers. For instance, if my boss speaks to one of my coworkers crossly, this might remind me of my alcoholic raging father, which brings up a slew of emotional discomfort—fear, anger, shame, etc.—and I therefore am triggered, even though my boss's tone has nothing at all to do with me in the present moment.

Unfortunately, triggers are unavoidable but not so the ways that we can learn to monitor and deal with them. Think about alcoholics driving past billboard ads for beer, scotch, and vodka. Think about drug addicts watching television crime dramas where people are selling or using drugs. Think about all of the attractive people (i.e., potential sexual partners) that a sex addict sees on a daily basis online and in real life. Then the roller coaster of life and the emotions that even an average day can induce. Triggers are everywhere, and there is nothing that addicts can do about that fact beyond learning to recognize and deal with them in healthy ways (a process discussed in detail in later chapters). For now, I will simply say that if an addict can learn to identify his or her triggers and stop them in their tracks—*before they induce undue craving*—then he or she has a much better chance to stay sober.

Understanding Escalation

JANET, A MARRIED, FORTY-YEAR-OLD TV PRODUCER with three teenage children, entered treatment for an intimacy disorder after her husband spotted her holding hands with another man in a local restaurant. Initially, she denied that she was romantically involved with that man, but then her husband asked to see her phone so he could read any text messages they'd exchanged. "I almost fell over from shock," she says, "because I suddenly realized the extent of my sexual behavior all there on my phone for my husband to see. It wasn't just the one guy, it was dozens of guys, and that was just since I'd cleared my phone's text history at the end of the previous month." Janet says that until that moment she literally had no conscious knowledge of how extensive her sexual acting-out had become.

She'd started out just flirting with strangers on social media, not meeting anyone in person. Eventually she'd agreed to meet one or two men for coffee, but she wasn't sexual with them. Then she had one small affair, so brief that it hardly counted (in her mind). Now she "found herself" having sex with at least 3 to 5 different men a month, and sometimes more.

Addicts of all types typically experience an increasing tolerance to the mood-altering effects of a pleasurable addictive substance or behavior. (Remember, the brain adjusts to excessive dopamine levels caused by continued use of addictive substances and behaviors by producing less dopamine and/or reducing the number of dopamine receptors in the brain.) As a result, addicts must, over time, use more of an addictive substance/behavior or a more intense substance/behavior to achieve and maintain the desired neurochemical high. Janet, in the example above, did both.

If you're struggling to understand this, consider drug addiction. Almost nobody shoots heroin right out of the gate. Instead, drug addicts ease into things by smoking marijuana or abusing a prescription medication. As time passes, their tolerance increases, and in response their habits escalate. Maybe they start smoking pot around the clock, or maybe they start popping pills by the handful, or whatever. Eventually, as their brain continues to adapt, even that level of usage doesn't get or keep them high the way they'd like. At some point many will "graduate" to drugs like cocaine, methamphetamine and heroin, and abuse these stronger substances in an effort to feel high (the way they used to). At first they might just sprinkle a bit of cocaine or meth into a joint or cigarette, or mix a tiny bit of heroin into the pills they've learned to crush and snort (for faster effect). In the end, without actually making a conscious decision to do so, they suddenly "find themselves" cooking and injecting their new drug of choice.

Sex addicts escalate their behavior in similar fashion. For instance, occasionally viewing and masturbating to generic (so-called "vanilla") online porn is by many people regarded as an enjoyable and relatively innocuous occasional activity, akin to drinking a few beers. However, *for some people* what begins as harmless recreation can become an all-consuming activity, pushing the user away from relationships, family, work, hobbies, and other life-affirming activities. Hours, even days are lost to sexual fantasy. Over time, the user may find that he or she is looking at and being turned on by increasingly more intense sexual imagery and/or extending their use into other sexual activities (webcam sex, casual sex, anonymous sex, and the like).

Common forms of escalation that occur with sexual addiction include (but are not even remotely limited to) the following:

- ✓ Serial affairs or multiple affairs at the same time
- ✓ High numbers of casual and/or anonymous sexual encounters
- ✓ Hours, sometimes even days, lost to pornography and/or other forms of online sexual behavior
- ✓ Alcohol and/or drug abuse concurrent with the sexual addiction
- ✓ Unsafe sex
- ✓ Sex with strangers or dangerous people
- ✓ Sex in dangerous locations
- ✓ Sensual massage, escorts and prostitution (buying or selling)
- ✓ Viewing illicit or unusual (for the addict) imagery
- ✓ Exhibitionism (either online or in person)
- ✓ Voyeurism (either online or in person)

For many sex addicts, escalation can involve a cross or co-occurring addiction.[5] These coexisting addictive disorders are discussed in a later chapter. For now, let's just say that sex addicts most common secondary addiction is to stimulant drugs like cocaine or methamphetamine.[6] These drugs cause feelings of euphoria, intensity, and power, along with the drive to obsessively do whatever activity the user wishes to engage in, including having sex, for extended periods. Some users say that meth, for instance, allows them to be sexual for an entire day, even two or three days, without sleeping, eating, or coming down—especially if an erection-enhancing drug like Viagra, Levitra, or Cialis is along for the ride. Sometimes meth is blatantly advertised on hookup and escort websites and apps: "Come over for PNP with me and my friend Tina." ("PNP" is shorthand for "party and play," indicating the person who posted this invitation is seeking both sex and drug use, and "Tina" is one of many common street names for meth.)

Alcohol, Recreational Drugs and Sex Addiction

Many people drink, some to excess, but most are not alcoholic. The problem with drinking alcohol for sex addicts (who are not alcoholics) is not necessarily that drinking is bad for you or that all sex addicts must refrain from substances of abuse. But the larger problem for sex addicts who drink and/or get high is simply this—when you consume mind-altering substances like alcohol, your resistance to "temptation" (of all kinds) decreases—at the same time as your level of impulsivity increases. Alcohol is a social lubricant. As such, it allows us to be more open, more verbal, and more engaged socially when drinking. When we drink, we are disinhibited, which may be a terrific state to be in when hanging out with friends after a long week to let off some steam, but not so much if you are going to end up alone afterward, slightly or even profoundly "buzzed," and thinking to yourself, *"Hey, what's the harm if I call up that xyz sexual experience?"* In this case, your "buzz", no matter how pleasant, also makes it harder to think through what you are about to do, and it discourages good decision-making when sexual decision-making is very important. Bottom line—in order to get the best leg up on early sexual recovery (at least in the first sixty to ninety days or so) it is best to avoid recreational drugs and alcohol during this time. However, if you find yourself unable to stop drinking and using, even though you have made a commitment to do so, you may need to consider if substance abuse might also be a problem.

Note that it is very helpful to observe the times when you feel like drinking or using (while you are not doing so), and if there is any correlation with a desire to get high and a desire to sexually act out. Some people become heavy drinkers/drug users in relationship to their sexuality, not so much because they are "sex addicts," but more because:

1) They have so much shame about their sexual desires (say same sex or transsexual interests) that they can't allow themselves to enjoy their sexual behaviors of choice without getting high. The high allows them to let go and have the kind of sex they truly enjoy. If your sexual behavior (non-offending) goes against your belief systems and you drink or drug in order to allow sex to be okay, this is something that needs to be discussed in detail with a professional. You may not be a sex addict, but you may have other issues with your sexuality and its relationship to drugs/alcohol that you will need to resolve

2) They have sex that they don't feel good about and then drink/use in order to feel better. There are some people who can only allow themselves to enjoy sexual behaviors that they don't themselves feel good about (bisexuality, kink, etc.). But then they can only tolerate the negative feelings brought up after sex by escaping via drugs and alcohol. If you find yourself

uncomfortable with your sexual desires and find yourself drinking/using after sex, then this, too, is something that needs to be discussed in detail with a professional.

As with other addictions, over time sexual addiction nearly always escalates in terms of time and/or content. And sooner or later, without intervention, these escalated behaviors result in profound and repeated negative life consequences. Over time, sex addicts neglect people important to them (children, spouses, friends), interests (recreation, self-care, creativity), and responsibilities (work, finances, family) to spend hours, sometimes even days, in a fantasy-based, emotionally elevated state of dissociation (the bubble/trance). And as their addiction escalates, their sexual activities often start going against their inherent values and beliefs (relationship fidelity, safer sex, not lying to or hurting others, etc.).

Understanding Denial

ALFONSO IS A THIRTY-FIVE-YEAR-OLD STRUCTURAL ENGINEER recently fired for using his company computer to view porn and for cruising for prostitutes during work hours. This happened after he'd already received a verbal reprimand from his boss, followed less than a month later by a written letter (entered into his work record) that very clearly told him what the consequences would be if his problematic behaviors reoccured at work. Now unemployed and deeply depressed, Alfonso still refuses to acknowledge or accept that his sexual behavior might be the cause or even a part of his problem. Instead, he sees sex as the "shining light" that keeps him from going over the edge. "Without the release of sex, I'd go crazy," he says. So instead of learning from his mistakes and seeing his sexual activity as the root of his many issues, he continues with his behaviors, all the while ruminating about how uptight his employer was about "perfectly normal guy stuff."

Active sex addicts rarely view their escapist sexual fantasies and behaviors *as the cause* of their unhappiness and life challenges. Even when neck deep in consequences, they somehow don't view their sexual acting out as a contributing factor. In fact, they typically see their behavior as the solution to rather than the cause of their emotional discomfort and various life problems. This is the face of denial. Put simply, sex addicts are nearly always out of touch with the costs of their addictive sexual behavior, at least until a major crisis hits. Prior to that, they ignore blatant warning signs, destroy relationships, breeze past workplace reprimands as well as related drug abuse, STDs (sexually transmitted diseases), unwanted pregnancies, financial problems, etc. They simply refuse to see or are unable to see the destructive effects of their sexual fantasies and behavior. Again, this is denial. In Alfonso's case, his denial is still in force even after a major sex-related work crisis.

Put simply, unlike *healthy individuals use past mistakes as a guide to future decision making,* while addicts choose to ignore past problems that are clearly related to their addictive behavior. In short, they place their compulsive search for sexual intensity at the top of their priority list without a second thought, no matter the cost. Instead of heeding the many warning signs of a serious problem, they rationalize, minimize, and justify their behavior, oftentimes blaming others for the consequences they face. For instance:

✓ If the police had been out chasing *real* criminals, I wouldn't have gotten caught up in that prostitution sting.

✓ If my wife wasn't such a cold fish, I wouldn't need to look at porn, and then I wouldn't have been fired from my job for misusing company equipment.

✓ If my husband hadn't gained so much weight, I wouldn't have lost interest in him and had so many affairs, and we wouldn't be divorced now.

For some sex addicts, denial is so deep that they somehow manage to stay blissfully unaware of the nature and extent of their problematic sexual behaviors, even when those behaviors escalate to the point of ruining their relationships and their lives. In short, they find ways to ignore the seriousness of their actions so they can continue with those actions, most often by blaming their poor decisions on someone or something outside of themselves. Denial for active addicts means externalizing the blame for their problems by making them someone or something else's fault. And this willful ignorance can go on for years. In fact, when confronted in the early stages of treatment with an adult-life sex and relationship history, many sex addicts are shocked to finally "discover" the extent and depth of their addictive behaviors.

The Evolutionary Underpinnings of Denial

Denial is actually a much-needed survival mechanism—an evolutionary imperative, if you will—that has developed over thousands of years. Consider our hunter/gatherer ancestors. If one of them was out foraging for food and a saber-tooth tiger attacked, and the full pain of a tiger bite was immediately experienced, this unlucky ancestor would have been completely unable to either fight back or flee and seek assistance. Instead, that individual would have simply shut down and become a tasty tiger treat. Luckily for our hypothetical ancestor, the ability to temporarily "deny" pain evolved, providing that person with a fighting chance at survival.

Let's view denial through a medical lens. If you've ever broken an arm or leg (or any other bone), then you know from experience that when the injury first occurs there is not a huge amount of pain. Mostly what you feel is surprise and disbelief. A few hours later, however, after you've been to the hospital to reset the bone so it can properly heal, the pain hits—*hard*—and even painkillers can't fully control it. We experience this delayed physical pain reaction because evolution has taught our brains to *temporarily ignore the pain* so we can keep it together long enough to seek help.

Our response to emotional pain works in exactly the same way. After a sudden emotional trauma like an unexpected death or tragedy, we tend to say things like, "No, this can't be," or, "It's not true," or, "This isn't happening." In other words, as humans we have the ability to temporarily deny the full extent of our emotional pain, just as we do with physical pain. Instead of being slammed with grief and becoming nonfunctional, our brains allow the pain to seep in gradually so that it doesn't overwhelm us.

Unfortunately, our denial can become twisted and abused for unhealthy purposes, in particular the maintenance of addictions.

Denial and Addiction

Denial is a complex series of internal lies and deceits. Typically, each fabrication is supported by one or more rationalizations, with each rationalization bolstered by still more falsehoods. When looked at objectively, denial is about as structurally sound as a house of cards in a stiff breeze, yet active addicts act and often feel like they are living in an impenetrable bomb shelter. They defend their flimsy lies and deceits with reckless abandon, no matter how ridiculous those lies actually are. In time, they start to believe their own lies, and they expect others to do so as well. And because addicts buy into their own dishonesty, their behaviors, no matter how crazy, can seem utterly reasonable to them. Yes, the rest of the world may easily see through the smokescreen, but addicts cannot (or will not). Instead they remain mired in the murky muck of their denial until their functional world devolves into a mess of addiction-related consequences.

Addicts never intend to destroy their relationships, hurt loved ones, or ignore their kids, or ruin their careers, or mangle their finances, or get arrested, or whatever. Yet they often end up in these very circumstances, arriving there incrementally as their denial escalates. Over time, they grow less able (and less willing) to see the connection between their increasing personal problems and their escalating addictive behaviors. Often deaf to the complaints, concerns, and criticisms of those around them—even those they profess to love—they will correspondingly devalue and dismiss (and/or blame) those who try to point out the problem. Instead of accepting that they may have a serious issue, they ignore attempted interventions and accuse others of nagging, being prudish and restrictive, not understanding them, or asking too much of them. They do this not because they truly don't care, but because they "need" to protect their addiction and because they are ashamed.

Denial Comes in Many Forms

As described in Chapter 1, the excitement and intensity of sexually addictive behavior creates for some people an extraordinarily powerful, self-induced, drug-like high (the bubble/trance). In order to protect unlimited access to this neurochemical high, sex addicts must find ways to rationalize and justify—to themselves and others—not just their actual sexual acting out but their physical and emotional unavailability. Unsurprisingly, sex addicts are incredibly creative in this regard, relying on a variety of techniques, including blame (also known as externalization), entitlement, justification, minimization, and rationalization.

Blame/Externalization: Frank, a thirty-year-old pilot, blames others. "With the lousy sex life I have at home, who wouldn't be looking at porn and chatting up women online for sex? Ever since we had kids, my wife doesn't have time for me. Plus, she's put on a lot of weight. It's like she got what she wanted (the kids), and now she feels like she doesn't have to worry about me anymore. Plus, even when we were having sex it was totally vanilla. She never wanted to try anything new or interesting, whereas some of the women I meet online are up for anything."

Entitlement: Jeff, a fifty-one-year-old executive who has received multiple written warnings about his use of porn at work, feels entitled. "Just look at how hard I am working. I give and give and give to this company. I work nights and sometimes even weekends, and it feels like there just isn't any time left for me. I deserve a little bit of pleasure in life. It can't be all work and no play. So if I spend a few hours here and there online, getting off on a little fantasy, that's a reward I deserve for all the work that I do."

Justification: Daniela, a twenty-four-year-old copywriter, justifies her behavior. "This is what single girls do. If I'm not in a relationship, then I need some kind of excitement. And all I'm doing is chatting up guys on social media, dating sites and a couple of apps. It's a lot better than sitting around in some cheesy bar waiting for some guy to buy me a drink. Plus, it gives me something to look forward to after work. It's exciting and distracting, and I don't even have to leave my apartment. And if some of those guys seem nice and want to come over for a quickie, there's nothing wrong with that. After all, if I was in a relationship I'd be having sex every night, so why can't I have sex every night when I'm not in a relationship?"

Minimization: Sam, a forty-four-year-old salesman, minimizes his behavior. "I'm no different than any other gay guy. All of us are on Grindr, waiting for our smartphone to buzz to let us know there's someone nearby who wants to have (mostly safe) sex. Everybody does it. We meet somebody online, we have sex, and then we brag about it the next day. Besides, I'm not in any danger. I'm a big boy and I can handle myself. And I can tell when someone is too weird or into drugs from the kinds of things they write me, so I don't get into those situations to begin with."

Rationalization: Suzanne, a thirty-six-year-old physician's assistant, rationalizes her behavior. "I'm not having real affairs like some of the other women I know. I'm not even flirting with the doctors at work, even though most of the nurses do. So if I go online for a few hours after my husband falls asleep at night and have my secret little intrigues, no one gets hurt and nothing comes of it. Lots of women are reading *Fifty Shades of Grey* and nobody thinks they're doing anything wrong, so why am I?"

On some level, even though their sexual behavior is likely harming not only themselves but their loved ones (and possibly others), many sex addicts somehow see themselves as the victim. This, too, is a form of denial. They say they feel overwhelmed and at the mercy of the people in their lives, and that sexual acting out gives them a sense of freedom and control that they do not otherwise experience. They view themselves as burdened by the seemingly unceasing demands of other people, especially those close to them, for attention, participation, validation, and support. Adding to their challenges, they find it difficult to identify their own emotional needs and nearly impossible to ask directly for those needs to be met in healthy ways.

Unfortunately, feeling like a victim (Poor Me) leads to feeling entitled (I Deserve) to act out, which of course leads back to engaging in problem sexual behavior. Even if sex addicts stop abusing sexual fantasies and behaviors to quell anxiety and cope with life, without some kind of outside help they will most likely find themselves searching for some other means of emotional escape, shifting from one addictive behavior to another. Typically, this "other means" manifests as either a cross or a co-occurring addiction. Unsurprisingly, denial works just as well for secondary addictions as primary addictions. The lies and deceits that sex addicts use to support their sexual acting out can also be used to support drinking, drugging, spending, binge eating, compulsive gambling, etc.

Denial Is Used Not Just by Addicts

Addiction (of all types) is sometimes referred to as a family disease because family members often co-sign and/or enable an addict's problematic behaviors. In such cases, family members are often as deeply in denial about the addiction and its consequences as the addict. This concept is discussed in more detail in later chapters. For now, it is important to state that denial (unconsciously working to to avoid the truth of a painful situation), whether by the addict or those around the addict, actually exacerbates the addict's desire to engage in escapist sexual behaviors. This is because denial is a complex series of lies and deceits that continually grows as the addiction escalates. The more complicated this web of deception becomes—and it gets incredibly complicated when family members are also pulled into it—the harder it is to sustain a façade of normalcy. Over time, the stress of building and maintaining denial can be exceedingly nerve-wracking for all parties involved. And, as you may recall, this type of distress is a primary trigger for setting the addictive cycle in motion. In this way, the addict's and/or the family's *system of denial* directly feeds the cycle of addiction.

Why Me? Understanding the Causes of Sexual Addiction

The first question anyone diagnosed with sexual addiction typically asks is pretty much the same: "How did I get this way?" and who could blame them? Ultimately, why a person is sexually addicted is less initially important than "how can I stop," which is the best place to begin therapy/treatment. Nevertheless, it is helpful to address the topic here, but only after noting the following: knowing *why* you are a sex addict will not cure or even control your sexual addiction, but it does often provide meaningful shame reduction, and even self-compassion.

Insight vs. Action in the Addiction Healing Process

ACTION OR EXPERIENCE	RESULT
• Gaining insight • Working on trauma • Psychodynamic psychotherapy • Understanding how past and present relate	↑ Insight ↑ Self-compassion ↓ Shame ↓ Self-hatred ↔ Sexual behaviors remain with little change
• Taking a history of past and present sexual behavior • Constructing a plan toward change • Actively engaging help from non-professionals in 12-step or faith-based groups • CBT and active forms of addiction therapy	↓ Problem sexual behaviors begin to stop in earnest ↑ Mood improves ↑ Hope ↓ Shame
Insight AND active steps	Ideal for personal growth AND behavior change

Nature Versus Nurture

MARK AND THOMAS, TWO MEN now in their mid-twenties, both discovered online porn when they were twelve-year-old best buddies. Both boys were from stable middle-class families in the same neighborhood. Both made good grades, played sports, and were starting to get interested in girls. One day after school Mark's older brother told them how they could access an online porn site. Curious and excited by what they might find, the two boys decided to look at porn for a short while before doing their homework.

In the days, months, and years that followed, Mark has occasionally viewed porn for sexual stimulation, but in no way, shape, or form would anyone say he is compulsive or obsessive with his use of pornography. Mostly he just logs on once in a while and quickly masturbates. And when he is dating someone he likes, he doesn't look at porn at all, preferring to stay focused on the actual woman in his life.

Thomas, on the other hand, after his first exposure to porn at age twelve, went home that very night and turned on the desktop computer in his room—a hand-me-down from his father's workplace—and cruised different porn sites for over an hour before going to bed. For him, this quickly became a regular pattern. By the time he was fourteen, he was looking at and masturbating to porn at least ten to twelve hours per week, sometimes more. His grades dropped, he isolated, he quit playing sports, and he lost interest in the girls at his school. In short, Thomas got addicted to pornography, and he experienced many of the usual consequences. Today, as an adult, his porn use is completely out of control and ruining his life. He can't keep a job, he hasn't dated since high school, he is having issues with erectile dysfunction, and he hates himself.

So why was Mark able to experiment with porn and move forward into a healthy life, when Thomas was addicted from almost the first image?

The simple truth is that some people are inherently vulnerable to addiction, and some people aren't. Consider alcohol. Nearly everyone tries alcohol at some point in his or her life, but only a small percentage of those folks become alcoholic. The same is true with other potentially addictive drugs and behaviors: many partake, but few become addicted. So why can some people try it and walk away when others cannot? Surely there must be some obvious, easily spotted difference between healthy people and potential addicts? Some telltale sign that's hard to miss? Right? *Wrong.*

Consider the example above. Mark and Thomas were so alike they were practically twins. They lived in the same neighborhood, they took the same classes, they earned the same grades, they played the same sports, and they hung out with the same kids. Heck, they even had the same haircut. From outward appearances, there was no way to know that one boy was predisposed to addiction while the other was not.

That said, there is a considerable amount of research into the causes of addiction, with scientists identifying two main categories of risk: nature and nurture.

Nature: Genetics and the Risk for Addiction

Dozens of studies have shown a link between genetic factors and susceptibility to addiction. Most of these studies focus on alcoholism, but it is not unreasonable to extend the findings to other addictions. For starters, various genetic mutations can either directly increase or decrease the risk for addiction, usually by altering the ways in which a particular substance (like alcohol) is experienced and processed in the body and brain.

In one study, scientists found that people who naturally have less reactivity to alcohol (as measured by body sway) are more likely to become alcoholic.[1] In other words, people who are genetically less susceptible to the negative side effects of alcohol can consume more longer (get higher) without falling down, getting sick, or passing out, and they are, as a result, more likely to drink alcoholically. Another study links a specific genetic variation affecting D2 dopamine receptors, which are part of the rewards center in the brain, to addiction. This genetic mutation, which essentially magnifies the pleasurable effects of addictive substances and behaviors, increases the risk not just for alcoholism, but for all other types of addiction.[2]

Genetic variations can also reduce the risk for addiction. For instance, it has long been known that people of East Asian ancestry are much less likely than other groups to become alcoholic. And scientists now know why. In short, they've identified a genetic mutation (prevalent in East Asian cultures) that causes a deficiency of the aldehyde dehydrogenase enzyme, which is critical to the metabolism of alcohol.[3] When alcohol is consumed by people with this genetic mutation, classic hangover symptoms (headache, dehydration, nerve and tissue sensitivity, rapid heartbeat, nausea, and the like) occur almost immediately. In other words, alcohol makes these folks physically ill instead of getting them high. Needless to say, alcoholism is incredibly rare among people with this genetic makeup.

Genetic factors can also contribute to addiction indirectly.[4] For instance, genetics are a factor in numerous psychiatric disorders: depression, anxiety, attention deficits, panic disorders, bipolar disorder, social phobia, etc. Not surprisingly, many people living with these disorders choose to *self-medicate* with alcohol, drugs, and/or intensely pleasurable behaviors. Over time this may become compulsive. In such cases, what is genetically inherited is not a unique response to a potentially addictive substance or behavior, but the propensity for vulnerability to addiction. For instance, people diagnosed with bipolar disorder are much more likely than others to also have a substance use disorder,[5] but this increased risk for addiction has nothing whatsoever to do with the ways in which addictive substances and behaviors are experienced in the body. Instead, it's connected to the person's desire and/or "need" to escape and dissociate from the shame and emotional pain of an underlying, genetically driven psychiatric disorder.

Other examples of the indirect effect of genetics on addiction are seen when we examine certain heritable personality traits such as impulsivity, risk taking, novelty seeking, and abnormal stress reactivity, all of which significantly increase the risk for addiction.[6] In short, the genetic predisposition toward rapid, unplanned actions and/or reactivity without regard to potential negative consequences is closely associated with addiction. Here, it is an inherited tendency toward certain character traits that cause dangerous behaviors, one of which may be the abuse of potentially addictive substances and/or behaviors that leads (indirectly) to addiction. Again, the effects are not related to the physical experience of the addictive substance or behavior; rather, the effects are part of a broad spectrum of psychological and emotional predispositions that incidentally increase the risk for addiction.

Epigenetics: The New Frontier

A relatively new field of study, known as *epigenetics*, will eventually impact addiction treatment. Essentially, epigenetics looks at the ways in which environmental factors can alter or even override the outcome of our genetic predispositions. For instance, in certain mice the agouti gene is linked with yellow fur and numerous health problems, including obesity and cancer. This gene, of course, is passed down through the generations, and with it comes the related propensity for health issues and shorter lives. However, if pregnant mice are fed certain dietary supplements, their offspring, even though they, too, carry the agouti gene, are much less susceptible to these health issues.[7] Though the external factor (dietary supplements) does not affect the mothers—they still have a much higher propensity for obesity and cancer—it does impact *genetic expression* in their offspring. Thus, it appears that genetics may not be a person's destiny in the way that we once thought. Perhaps in time, as scientists gain more detailed knowledge of the relationship between genetics and various forms of addiction, we may develop epigenetic methods of preventing and/or combatting these disorders.

Nurture: Environment and the Risk for Addiction

Research tells us that we can't blame addiction entirely on genetic susceptibility; environmental factors also play a significant role. But how big a role is this, and how can we measure it? One way that scientists have separated nature from nurture in addiction causation studies is by studying the incidence of addiction among adopted children and twins (especially identical twins who were separated at birth and raised by different sets of parents). In this way, the relative influence of genetic risk factors versus environmental risk factors can be measured.

Adoption studies typically ask: what happens to the children of alcoholics if they're adopted into a family where neither parent abuses alcohol? Researchers have consistently found that people with biological, (not adoptive) parents who were alcoholics are much more likely to develop alcoholism.[8] So score a point for genetics. Of course, being more likely to develop alcoholism doesn't mean that alcoholism is an absolute certainty. In fact, lots of people in these studies were not alcoholic. Plus, plenty of biological children of non-alcoholics do become alcoholic. So now we can score a few points for environmental influences.

Comparable studies have been conducted for cocaine, nicotine, and opiates with remarkably similar results,[9] leading scientists to conclude that somewhere between 40 and 70 percent of the risk for addiction is genetic, and somewhere between 60 and 30 percent is environmental. If we wanted to use the center point of those estimates, we could say that *the risk for addiction is 55 percent genetic and 45 percent environmental*. In addition to this relatively even distribution of blame, it appears that nature can easily be usurped by nurture (again potentially epigenetics). For instance, abused and/or neglected children have an incredibly high risk for addiction (and other adult-life psychological issues) regardless of genetic influences.

Furthermore, the more times a child is traumatized, the greater the likelihood of adverse reactions, such as addiction, later in life. One study found that survivors of chronic childhood trauma (four or more significant trauma experiences prior to age eighteen) are:

> 1.8 times as likely to smoke cigarettes
> 1.9 times as likely to become obese
> 2.4 times as likely to experience ongoing anxiety
> 3.6 times as likely to be depressed
> 3.6 times as likely to qualify as promiscuous
> 7.2 times as likely to become alcoholic
> 11.1 times as likely to become an intravenous drug user.[10]

Another relatively common environmental risk factor is early exposure to an addictive substance or behavior. Numerous studies have found that the lower the age of first use, the higher the likelihood of addiction.[11] This is true with all forms of addiction, including sexual addiction. Whether sex was vilified or glorified, a large percentage of sex addicts were exposed to it at an unusually early age.[12] One recent survey of adult sex addicts found that 41 percent were using pornography before the age of twelve.[13] Keep in mind the fact that when today's adult sex addicts were twelve or younger, Internet porn was not nearly as accessible as it is today, so kids had to look hard for it, or, more likely, they had to be inadvertently or intentionally exposed to it—a potentially traumatic experience either way. (Nowadays the *average* age of first exposure to pornography is eleven.[14] *Yikes!* More about teens and sexual addiction in our online bonus book resource section, which can be downloaded at *hcibooks.com*.)

Sometimes the age of first use (drugs or behaviors) and familial instability (including a family history of mental illness and/or addiction) are directly related, as addictive substances and/or activities are readily available within the home. In such cases, the other environ-mental risk factors (abuse, neglect, inconsistent parenting, etc.) may be the overarching factor in the development of addiction.

Trauma and Addiction

There is an undeniable link between childhood trauma and numerous adult-life symptoms and disorders, including addiction.

My esteemed colleague, Dr. Christine Courtois, provides a brief definition of trauma in her new book, *It's Not You, It's What Happened to You*, writing, "Trauma is any event or experience (including witnessing) that is physically and/or psychologically overwhelming to the exposed individual."[15] Dr. Courtois also notes that trauma is highly subjective. In other words, incidents that might be highly trau-matizing to one person may be humdrum for another.[16] For instance, a fender-bender might be much more traumatic for a new mother with her baby in the car than say for a professional race car driver.

There are many types of trauma as can be seen below:

Impersonal trauma: acts of God such as natural disasters, being in the wrong place at the wrong time, etc.

Interpersonal trauma: intentional acts by other people, such as abuse, neglect, inappropriate enmeshment, assault, robbery, etc.

Identity trauma: based on the victim's inherent characteristics, such as gender, ethnicity, sexual orientation, etc.

Community trauma: based on the victim's membership in a par-ticular community, such as a family, tribe, religion, etc.[17]

Sadly, for many people the experience of trauma is chronic, that is—repeated and layered over time. This is often referred to as *complex trauma*. Complex trauma is especially problematic when it occurs within early family life, which is an interpersonal trauma subtype known as *attachment trauma*. Complex (chronic) attachment trauma is highly postively correlated with addictions of all types, but shows up with high frequency particularly among sex and love addicts.

> DENISE, A TWENTY-FIVE-YEAR-OLD MARKET ANALYST, grew up the only daughter of two alcoholics. Her father sexually abused her from a very young age, and her mother abused her verbally, emotionally, and sometimes physically. The abuse was always worse when they drank. Now, as an adult, Denise is struggling to hold on to a job, to maintain her friendships, and to control her sexual behavior. She says that every evening after work she logs on to half a dozen or so hookup apps and chats with men seeking sex. More often than not, she has sex with two or three different men by the end of a given night. As soon as one man leaves her apartment, she's online looking for the next one. Most nights she is awake and acting out sexually until three or four in the morning, leaving her both tired and unpro-ductive the next day at work, which is an issue that may soon get her fired. Deeply ashamed of her behavior, she nevertheless continues to engage in it, stating that it's the only thing that makes her feel impor-tant and alive. At this point, she's at a loss to explain her actions. She has no way of knowing or understanding that her compulsive adult sexual responses to any and all forms of emotional discomfort are in fact learned coping mechanisms that are relatively normal (or at least expected) given the degree and nature of the complex attachment trauma she experienced in childhood. Without this understanding, she simply sees herself as dirty, unworthy of love, and hopelessly broken.

Sadly, without some form of therapy or intervention, individuals like Denise often don't make the connection between their child-hood trauma and their adult-life sexual problems. Due to this lack of understanding and association, many of these folks think of them-selves as "broken" or simply as "bad people," using their adult-life sexual acting out as proof of how unlovable they really are. *They simply don't understand that their upbringing was lacking and left them without a positive sense of self or needed life skills, and that their problematic sexual behaviors are an adaptive response to what they experienced.*

The simple truth is addicts of all types typically report multiple instances and forms of early-life neglect, abuse, shame, and family dysfunction.[18] In one survey asking sex addicts about their childhoods, 97 percent reported emotional abuse, 83 percent reported sexual abuse, and 71 percent reported physical abuse.[19] In another survey, 38 percent reported emotional abuse, 17 percent reported sexual abuse, and 16 percent reported physical abuse.[20] Obviously, that's a wide variance between studies. Numerous factors may account for the variation in findings, and most likely the real numbers lie somewhere in the middle. Either way, it is clear that an abnormally large percentage of sex addicts were traumatized in childhood.

Put simply, addicts nearly universally report early-life complex attachment trauma: neglect, abuse, inconsistent parenting, and/or other forms of family dysfunction.[21] Basically, their developmental and dependency needs are not met in childhood they walk around their world feeling like they have a "hole in their soul," as one addict put it. So we see that addicts are most often people who've been emotionally wounded, usually early and repeatedly, in ways that leave them feeling unworthy of love, affection, connection, and happiness. They end up with a distorted, *deeply shame-based* sense of self, where every negative or problematic experience serves as a reminder that they, themselves are defective and unlovable. And when that's the message bouncing around in a person's head, it's understandable that he or she might consistently and repeatedly choose to self-medicate and/or self-soothe with drugs, alcohol, and/or a pleasurable behaviors, in time becoming emotionally and psychologically dependent on these temporary (feel good) external fixes.

Sexual Abuse, Sexual Shame, and Sexual Addiction

Without doubt, childhood sexual abuse, whether a single incident or chronic, leaves its victims with feelings of both confusion and shame. This is true whether the abuse is *overt*, meaning "hands-on," or *covert*, as occurs when a parent "emotionally partners" with a child (see the next section for further information).[22] Exacerbating matters is the fact that childhood sexual abuse is often coupled with other forms of early-life trauma, such as emotional, psychological, and/or physical neglect and abuse,[23] creating layers of traumatic experience and various forms of shame—though sexual shame is nearly always the most powerful.

Oftentimes sexually shamed children begin to self-medicate their emotional discomfort relatively early in life, usually during adolescence but sometimes even before. After all, body image issues, shame about being looked at and/or touched inappropriately, and feeling "icky" about too much trust and affection can all begin *very early* in childhood. It is is typical to see these emotionally challenged children seeking solace (by early adolescence), via drug and alcohol abuse. That said, many children also learn (or are taught) that they can self-soothe with sexual behaviors (including sexual fantasy and masturbation), usually by eroticizing and reenacting some aspect of their sexual trauma. In fact, self-soothing through eroticized reenactment of trauma is relatively common.[24]

Unfortunately, though distracting in the moment, these self-soothing sexual behaviors tend to exacerbate preexisting shame and emotional discomfort, thus creating an even greater need for escape and dissociation. As such, many deeply sexually shamed "sexual trauma survivors" find themselves mired in an addictive cycle of self-hatred and sexual shame, ameliorated by sexual fantasy and activity, followed by still more self-hatred and sexual shame. In short, their escapist addictive sexual fantasies and behaviors automatically and inherently trigger the need for more of the same. This, as you may recall from Chapter 1, is the basis of the sex-addiction cycle.

Understanding Covert Incest

Covert incest, also known as *emotional* incest is the indirect, sexualized and/or romanticized emotional use/abuse of a child by a parent, stepparent, or any other long-term caregiver.[25] In contrast to *overt sexual abuse*, which involves hands-on sexual contact, *covert abuse involves* less direct forms of sexuality—sexuality that is emotionally implied or suggested rather than overtly acted out. In this way, a child is used for parental emotional fulfillment, forced to support the adult by serving as a trusted confidante and/or an "emotional spouse." Though there may be little to no direct sexual activity, these overly enmeshed relationships have a sexualized undertone, with the parent expressing overly graphic verbal interest in the child's physical development and sexual characteristics and/or betraying the child's boundaries through voyeurism, exhibitionism, sexualized conversations, and inappropriate sharing of intimate stories and/or images.

Covert incest often occurs when parents have distanced themselves from one another both physically and emotionally, and one or the other parent begins to place their adult emotional needs on their child, using the child as a kind of surrogate partner. Some parents may tie their own self-esteem to the academic, sports or other success by the child. Either way, the child's developmental needs tend to be ignored, and emotional growth (especially in the area of healthy sexual and romantic attachment) can be profoundly stunted. Often, the perpetrating adult is usually completely unaware of the emotional damage he or she is creating by using their child as an emotional object, rather than turning to other adults for support. And typically for many trauma survivors without concrete, identifiable trauma stories (involving: hitting, rape, profound neglect, violence etc.), this kind of emotional damage can be hard to identify. Clients in treatment will say things like, "Once Dad left, I got all of Mom's attention, she was with me constantly and told me everything." They often feel like they got a pretty good deal, but in reality being responsible for a parent's emotional needs at such a young age can be very damaging to a child and bodes poorly for their future relationships and sexuality.

Dashiell, a thirty-three-year-old CPA raised in an upper-middle class household, says that for many years, before his much younger sister was born, his mom would pull him out of school some days, simply because she wanted his company. She just dragged him along while she shopped, and then they'd have lunch, with Dash listening to his mom talk about her life with his dad and how she felt about that relationship. Sometimes she would take Dash to the movies with her—not kid movies, but grown-up stuff. He says that his dad was always either working or drinking, and his mom didn't have many women friends, so he was her fill-in. "In a way, it wasn't so bad. I liked skipping school and eating out and getting to see movies that other kids didn't, but at the same time I always felt a bit weird with her. She always seemed to sit a little too close to me, and she commented on my body all the time, especially when I was a teenager. And sometimes she'd walk into the bathroom when I was in the shower to put away towels or some stupid thing that could easily have waited until I was done and dressed. Lots of stuff like that. I had no privacy. Even if I was in my room with the door locked she would be right outside, listening and asking me through the closed door what I was doing, was I okay, did I need her for anything. All I really wanted was for her to leave me alone. Sometimes she would undress in front of me asking me to help "choose her outfit" while walking around half naked. What I find confusing even now, is that she never actually touched me sexually. Still, by the time I was fifteen or sixteen, just being in the same room with her made my skin crawl." Now in his early thirties,

Dash is struggling with sexual addiction, compulsively hooking up with women via apps like Tinder and Ashley Madison, at all hours of the day and night. His relationship with his mother, feeling out of control, set the template for future sexual intimacy as having to take place where he does feel a sense of control (emotional safety)—with prostitutes or casual affairs.

The mixed feelings Dash has about adult intimacy are not uncommon in covert incest survivors. On the one hand, his special relationship with his mother was a cherished privilege; on the other hand, something about it felt icky and wrong. Most covert incest survivors initially resist the notion that they have been sexually abused because they were never actually touched in a sexual way by the perpetrator. However, these relationships are indeed sexualized. Essentially, a child in these circumstances is sexualized and treated as an adult partner, and therefore he or she is deprived of healthy attachment bonds, stable emotional growth, and many other basics of childhood development. In lieu of healthy development, the child is taught that his or her value is based not on who he or she is as a person, but on how much he or she can please, amuse, and/or bond with the caretaker. As a result, covert incest survivors typically respond in the same ways as survivors of overt (hands-on) sexual abuse, with many of the following adult-life symptoms and consequences:

- ✓ Characterlogical and personality (ego) problems
- ✓ Addiction and/or compulsivity
- ✓ Difficulty developing and maintaining long-term intimacy
- ✓ Narcissism and angry emotional reactivity
- ✓ Shame and feelings of inadequacy
- ✓ Dissociation
- ✓ Difficulties with self-care (emotional and/or physical)
- ✓ Love/hate relationships, especially with spouses and family

✓ Inappropriate bonding or overly distancing with their own
child (intergenerational abuse)
✓ Adult intimacy disorders

As pervasive and damaging as covert incest is, it frequently goes
unrecognized even in treatment therapy settings. As my colleague
Debra Kaplan puts it, "The obvious signs are obscured from plain
view. It is like the air in the room—it's here, but you can't see it."[26]
This confusion affects survivors and therapists alike. In general, the
thinking seems to be that if there's no actual physical sexual contact, then no harm has been done. It is only when we dig beneath
the surface that we see the connections between covertly incestuous
behaviors and adult intimacy and addiction issues, including sexual
addiction.

Sexual Addiction: The Perfect Storm

Sex addicts, like all other addicts, are subject to a combination of
genetic and environmental risk factors. For instance, a combination
of genetic predisposition, abusive, alcoholic, or mentally ill parents,
childhood trauma, and early exposure occurs relatively often, creating a witch's brew of ongoing life problems: not just addiction, but
numerous other social, emotional, and psychological issues. Given
this, it is clear that any discussion about the possible causes of sexual
addiction is not so much an argument of nature versus nurture as
an examination of how the two factors come together to influence
individual behavior and response. In short, addictive disorders of all
types, sexual addiction included, are driven by genetics and environmental factors. When early-life sexual trauma (overt or covert) is part
of the mix, the odds of sexual addiction versus another addiction are
greatly increased.

5

Cybersex and Porn Addiction

JASON, A THIRTY-YEAR-OLD SELF-EMPLOYED electrician, is a soon-to-be divorced father of two young children. He says that after his kids were born, his wife was always either too tired for sex or just plain not interested in it. When he complained about this to a fellow electrician he'd known for a number of years, his friend suggested that he check out the Tinder hookup app. Before long, he had profiles on five different apps, and he was spending more time hooking up with strangers than managing his shop. Within a year, he had fallen behind on the mortgage and in paying his many suppliers. "I started lying to my wife, too, telling her I was working late when I was really hooking up." Eventually, his wife got suspicious and checked his phone to see what she could find. And she found quite a lot. "There were nude pictures of me and a lot of the women I was hooking up with and text messages setting up all sorts of encounters. And that was it for her. She immediately took our kids and left me. Now she wants a divorce. The worst part is that even with all this pain, and her hurt, I still can't stay away from those apps."

I n the twenty-first century, digital technology is omnipresent. At this point, nearly everyone in modern Western culture either owns or has easy access to a computer, laptop, tablet, pad, smartphone, or some other Internet-enabled digital device. As a result, we now have 24/7, anytime, anywhere access to information, entertainment, and social interaction—with much of that material and interconnectivity being sexual in nature. Today, nearly a billion people daily log onto Facebook and similar social media on a daily basis to catch up with family, friends, and to stay connected. For the vast majority of people, this is not an issue. They are able to play with and enjoy cybersexual activity in healthy ways, without becoming addicted or experiencing negative consequences, just as most people are able to casually enjoy things like alcohol, gambling, video gaming, and recreational drugs without becoming addicted or experiencing major problems. However, for people vulnerable to addiction and psychological disorders, *sexnology* (i.e., sexual technology) can be as much a danger zone as any other potential addiction.

As a therapist who primarily treats sex and romance addicts, I initially noticed tech-related issues in the early 1990s, when online bulletin boards (BBS) and porn sites first hit the web. Prior to that, my clients were mostly hooked on real-world sexuality: serial affairs, prostitutes, sex clubs, and adult movie theaters, plus the occasional guy hooked on phone sex (the old-fashioned kind of phone that plugged into the wall). But when home computers and ubiquitous Internet connections came along, my clients were suddenly and primarily engaging in tech-driven sexuality. And this tech-sex trend continues unabated, with current-day sex addicts hooked on digital pornography, virtual sex games, webcam sex, hookup apps, *teledildonics* (devices that offer a long-distance imitation of mutual sex), and whatever else R&D departments can dream up.

Furthermore, as both scientific research and anyone who's been treating sex addicts for more than a decade can tell you, with every advance in digital technology, more and more people are challenged by sexual addiction. Consider that studies conducted in the 1980s (pre-Internet) generally suggested that anywhere from 3 to 5 percent of the adult male population was sexually addicted.[1] By 1999—still the very early days of Internet usage—that percentage had approximately doubled, to 8.5 percent.[2] Fifteen years later we don't have an updated percentage from researchers, but anecdotal evidence strongly suggests the number is still climbing. Either way, it is clear that digital technology both leads to and facilitates sexual addiction. In short, as digital technology has increased our highly affordable, mostly anonymous, nearly instant access to potentially addictive sexual imagery, activity, and partners, sexual addiction has become more problematic and widespread. Today, it would be difficult to find even a single sex addict who hasn't been involved in some way with sex online, as it is just *so easy* to access.

Cybersex Variations

Online porn is the "industry leader" when it comes to cybersex addiction. This is hardly a surprise, given the recent online porn explosion. And no, I'm not exaggerating when I use the word *explosion*. In their 2011 book, *A Billion Wicked Thoughts*, researchers Ogi Ogas and Sai Gaddam write:

IN 1991, THE YEAR THE WORLD WIDE WEB WENT ONLINE, there were fewer than 90 different adult magazines published in America, and you'd have been hard-pressed to find a newsstand that carried more than a dozen. Just six years later, in 1997, there were about 900 pornography sites on the Web. Today, the filtering software CYBERsitter blocks 2.5 *million* adult Web sites.[3]

Of course, pornography is merely the tip of the "sexnological" iceberg. In today's world it is possible to meet someone on a dating site or a hookup app, to flirt with that person via text and sext, to have virtual sex with that person via webcam, and then brag about this hot new relationship on social media—all without ever being in the same room with that person (or even the same country).

Hookup apps in particular are problematic for addicts, primarily because they present an entire universe of readily available potential sexual partners, helpfully arranged, thanks to geo-locating software, from nearest to farthest away. And a person's marital status, hobbies, job, religion, goals, and worldview don't matter on these apps because they're all about the quick encounter. No muss, no fuss, just the sex, thank you very much. Many cybersex addicts, such as Jason in the example above, post profiles on multiple apps simultaneously, staying logged in to all of them 24/7, checking them constantly. Some looking for the next sexual encounter before they're even done with the current one.

Sexual Evolution?

1985: MICHELLE, A SINGLE TWENTY-EIGHT-YEAR-OLD events planner, was feeling lonely one evening. Hoping to meet Mr. Right (or at least Mr. Right Now) she showered, did her hair, put on makeup, spritzed herself with perfume, and put on a slinky black dress. Then she walked downstairs from her second-floor apartment, hailed a cab, and took an expensive ride to a singles bar on the other side of town (not wanting any of her friends or neighbors to see her and figure out what she was up to). At the club, she bought herself a couple of overpriced drinks and waited for a decent-looking guy to display interest in her. Several men offered to buy her a drink, but none of them was her type. Eventually, dejected and depressed, she left the bar and took the long cab ride home.

2016: MICHELLE, A SINGLE TWENTY-EIGHT-YEAR-OLD events planner, was feeling lonely one evening. Hoping to meet Mr. Right (or at least Mr. Right Now), she pushed some popcorn into the microwave and logged on to her Tinder smartphone app. She noticed a cute guy right away. She swiped his profile to indicate interest, and before her microwave popcorn was ready she was texting with him. Twenty minutes later he arrived at her doorstep, happy to share her popcorn, a movie, and a little bit more. No hours of preparation, no expensive cab ride or overpriced drinks, no parade of losers, no sore feet and ankles from standing around in high heels for three hours, and no disappointment at the end of the night. "Cute guy" was gone by 11:00 PM (in time for her to catch the late news) at her request. Easy!

In today's digital world, Michelle benefits from the Internet's "Triple-A Engine"[4]: Accessibility, Affordability, and Anonymity. For twenty-first century Michelle, digital technology removed the barriers to romance and sexuality that once existed. Thus the incredibly limited *across-town* dating pond of yesteryear is now transformed into a veritable ocean of opportunity. Instead of wasting her night, hoping to get laid, she quickly and easily located the connection she was seeking. And she is hardly alone in her approach.

In today's world, practically everyone who's interested in meeting a potential romantic or sexual partner is looking online. Men and women, gay and straight, young and old—they are all searching for someone, and they're nearly always conducting that search in the digital universe. And this is hardly a U.S.-based or even an English language phenomenon. For instance, eHarmony, a dating website launched in 2000, now has members in 150 different countries.[5] And the dating *websites* that dominated the mid-2000s currently seem like antiquated small potatoes. In fact, the online romance and sex scene didn't truly take flight until 2009, with the advent of dating and hookup *apps*.

The first dating/hookup app was Grindr, geared toward gay men seeking sex and/or romance (but mostly sex). Almost immediately that app went wild, and within a few short months of its launch the marketplace was littered with knockoffs geared toward every demographic imaginable. These days, whatever it is that you're looking for, there's an app that will help you find it. And an astounding number of people are taking advantage. For instance, Tinder, a relative latecomer to the "adult friend finder" scene (launched in August 2012), in 2015 has more than 50 million users, and they're swiping at other members' profiles 1.5 billion times per day.[6] (That's "billion, not million, per day," not year.) People today searching online for romantic and sexual content and contacts aren't tethered to an actual computer, as mobile devices are more functional—maybe even preferable—when it comes to online dating and mating.

Put simply, the amount and variety of intensely sexually arousing imagery and activity now available via digital devices is nearly endless, with new sexnologies (and for addicts, new forms of sexual acting out) arise almost daily. And thanks to the advertising-based business model initially employed by newspapers, TV, and radio, nearly all of this sexual content and activity is either free or low-cost, meaning almost anyone can instantly, affordably, and relatively anonymously access this endless stream of sexual content and potential partners 24/7/365.

Cybersex addicts find the anonymity that can be obtained online especially appealing, as it lets them be sexual in ways that do not put them at risk for arrest, shame, public embarrassment, and other consequences, as did many of yesteryear's analog sexual environments with less risk of discovery (and therefore intervention) by spouses or others who may be affected by their addiction. Thanks to the anonymity and secrecy provided by digital technology, cybersex addicts can find and experience about anything they want online—without their families, friends, employers, neighbors, or anyone else in their lives knowing what they're up to.

What Is Cybersex?

The most typical online/social media driven sexual behaviors are listed below. NOTE that being involved with any one or more than one of them, even on a regular basis, is not indicative of a problem, but when these experiences are abused to the point where they become all-consuming, interfering with day-to-day life, their abuse indicates evidence of a clear problem:

- ✓ Casual and/or anonymous sexual hookups facilitated by dating, prostitution, and hookup websites, and apps
- ✓ Sexting, texting sexual content and/or video sex chats
- ✓ Searching for sexualized imagery and/or potential sex partners on social media sites
- ✓ Sexting (sending and receiving overt sexual images) with or without masturbation
- ✓ Seeking (or selling) sexual favors via websites like Craigslist and Backpage, and also on more traditional dating and hookup websites and apps
- ✓ Searching for and hooking up with PNP (party and play) partners via websites and apps (drugs and sex)
- ✓ Seeking and engaging in marathon sex and/or group sex, with partners found via websites and apps
- ✓ Online exhibitionism and voyeurism via webcam, often on chat sites that randomly pair chat partners (such as Chatroulette and Omegle)

✓ Teledildonic masturbatory devices that warm, lubricate, pulse, and grip in tandem with sexual activities taking place onscreen (such as porn videos or even via live webcam performances)

✓ Virtual-reality sex games that allow users to create customized fantasy avatars (animated selves) then used to participate in interactive online sexcapades

✓ Online porn in all forms: webcam, video, anime, prostitution, images, etc.

The Face of Pornography Addiction

FRANKLIN IS A SINGLE, TWENTY-EIGHT-YEAR-OLD insurance claims adjustor. Every morning he wakes up and the first thing he does is masturbate to online pornography. He actually keeps his iPad on the nightstand next to his bed for easy access. As Franklin's day progresses, so does his porn use. He even watches porn on his iPhone while he's driving. "I actually love looking at videos in the car because it feels dangerous and forbidden, and that adds to the excitement. Sometimes I even masturbate while I'm driving." He admits that he's gotten several tickets for erratic driving but says he's always managed to switch his phone off and zip up before a police officer or anyone else can actually catch him in the act. After work, Franklin usually orders pizza or takeout Chinese from a place near his apartment, and then he watches several hours of porn beamed wirelessly from his iPad to his 55-inch flat-screen TV. "My goal is always to find the one perfect video that I haven't seen before," he says. "And usually even a so-so new video is better than a really good one that I've seen a few times." On an average day, Franklin spends at least three or four hours looking at and masturbating to digital pornography. Sadly, most days his entire compliment of social interaction occurs solely at either work or while buying food. As such he can go long periods without any other kind of live human connection at all.

The Internet is rife with porn of every ilk imaginable, and people of every age, race, religion, gender and sexual orientation are viewing it. Research suggests that approximately *12 percent of all websites offer pornographic content*, and *35 percent of all downloads involve erotic content*.[7] And frankly, the amount of currently available (mostly free) online porn increases by the minute, thanks primarily to user-generated imagery (sexts, webcam mutual masturbation sessions, etc.) Furthermore, the barriers to accessing porn that once existed—cost, proof of age, etc.—are no longer in play. Today, all a person who's interested in porn needs to do is find a porn site and start clicking. So it's hardly a surprise that porn addiction is among the most common forms of sex/cybersex addiction.

Many porn addicts couple their porn use with compulsive masturbation and/or various forms of non-intimate partner sex such as webcam sex, sexting, anonymous sex, casual sex, affairs, use of prostitutes, exhibitionism, voyeurism, etc. That said, porn addiction is often a stand-alone form of compulsive sexuality.

Generally speaking, porn addiction occurs when an individual consistently loses control over whether he or she views and uses pornography, the amount of time he or she spends with pornography, and the types of pornography that he or she uses. Research suggests that in today's world most porn addicts spend *at least* eleven or twelve hours per week looking at (and usually masturbating to) pornography, most often digital imagery accessed via their computer, laptop, tablet, smartphone, or some other Internet-enabled device![8] (Magazines, VHS tapes, DVDs, and other "traditional" forms of pornography are still in use, but the vast majority of porn addicts prefer the anonymity, affordability, and 24/7/365 accessibility that digital technologies provide.) And this eleven or twelve hours per week number is the *low* end of the spectrum. Many porn addicts devote double or even triple that amount of time to their addiction.

Common signs that casual porn use has escalated to the level of addiction include:

- ✓ Continued level of porn use remains unchanged despite consequences and/or promises made to self or others to stop
- ✓ Escalating amounts of time spent on porn use
- ✓ Hours, sometimes even days, lost to searching for, viewing, and organizing pornography
- ✓ Masturbation to the point of abrasions or injury
- ✓ Viewing progressively more arousing, intense, or bizarre sexual content
- ✓ Lying about, keeping secrets about, and covering up the nature and extent of porn use
- ✓ Anger or irritability if asked to stop using porn
- ✓ Reduced or even nonexistent interest in real-world sex and relationship intimacy
- ✓ Male sexual dysfunction (erectile dysfunction, delayed ejaculation, inability to reach orgasm)
- ✓ Deeply rooted feelings of loneliness, longing and/or detachment
- ✓ Drug/alcohol abuse in combination with porn use
- ✓ Drug/alcohol addiction relapse related to porn use or feelings about porn use
- ✓ Increased objectification of strangers, viewing them as body parts rather than people
- ✓ Escalation from viewing two-dimensional images to using the Internet for casual/anonymous sexual hookups, paid sex, etc.

Sadly, porn addicts are often reluctant to seek help because they don't view their hidden, often shameful solo sexual behaviors as an underlying source of their unhappiness. And when they do seek assistance, they often seek help with addiction-related symptoms—depression, loneliness, and relationship troubles—rather than the porn problem itself. Many attend psychotherapy for extended periods without ever discussing (or even being asked about) pornography or masturbation. Either it feels too shameful to them to even talk about, or they simply don't see the correlation between their porn use and the problems they're having in life. As such, their core problem remains underground and untreated.

Porn-Induced Sexual Dysfunction

As you may have noticed in the above list of potential consequences of porn addiction, male porn addicts sometimes experience sexual dysfunction related to their porn abuse. In fact, erectile dysfunction (ED), delayed ejaculation (DE), and inability to reach orgasm (anorgasmia) are all increasingly documented consequences of pornography abuse. One 2012 survey of 350 self-identified sex addicts found that 26.7 percent reported issues with sexual dysfunction.[9] Similar studies, smaller in scale, show comparable results. One such study, looking at twenty-four male sex addicts, found that one in six (16.7 percent) reported erectile dysfunction.[10] Another, this one looking at nineteen male sex addicts, found that eleven of the nineteen (58 percent) reported some form of sexual dysfunction.[11]

Put simply, growing numbers of physically healthy men, including men in their sexual prime, are suffering from sexual dysfunction—typically with real partners rather than with porn—and their dysfunction is directly related to their abuse of online pornography. Furthermore, this issue is not entirely due to the frequency of masturbation and orgasm outside a primary relationship (i.e., the need for a sexual refractory period in which males "reload," so to speak). In reality, the problem is increasingly related to the fact that when a man spends 70, 80, or even 90 percent of his sexual life masturbating to online porn—endless images of sexy, exciting, constantly chang-ing partners and experiences—he is, over time, likely to find his real partner(s) less sexually stimulating than the visuals parading through his mind. As such, the digital porn explosion has created in some men an *emotional/psychological disconnection that is manifesting physically as sexual dysfunction* with real partners.

In their paper, "Evaluation and Treatment of Sex Addiction," Kenneth Paul Rosenberg, Patrick Carnes, and Suzanne O'Connor state the matter rather clearly, writing that "Sex addiction patients are generally not good at sex. They function poorly in the bedroom. Sex addicts feverishly pursue their dysfunctional sexual behaviors yet generally have sexual difficulties with intimate partners.... Premature ejaculation, erectile dysfunction [and] anorgasmia ... are common."[12] And this is most apparent when sex addicts are hooked primarily on pornography.[13]

Possible signs of porn-induced male sexual dysfunction include:

- ✓ A man is able to achieve erections and orgasms with pornog-raphy, but he struggles with one or both when he's with a real-world partner.
- ✓ A man is able to have sex and achieve orgasm with real-world partners, but reaching orgasm takes a long time and his part-ners complain that he seems disengaged.
- ✓ A man is able to maintain an erection with real-world partners, but he can only achieve orgasm by replaying porn clips in his mind.
- ✓ A man increasingly prefers pornography to sex with a real part-ner, finding it more intense and more engaging.

The simple, sad truth is that, thanks to heavy porn use, growing numbers of men are suffering from sexual dysfunction, be it ED, DE, and/or anorgasmia. Even worse, male sexual dysfunction affects not just men, but their romantic partners. After all, if a guy can't get it up, keep it up, or reach orgasm, then his partner's sexual pleasure is also likely to be diminished.

Sex Addiction Is Sex Addiction, No Matter Where You Play

It is important to note that the basics of sexual addiction are the same with or without the involvement of technology. Put simply, cybersex addicts engage in their problematic sexual behaviors repeatedly and compulsively, despite clearly related negative life consequences. As a result, their relationships (should they have them) are threatened, school and work become a struggle, and they lose interest in recreation, hobbies, and other activities they used to enjoy. Cybersex addicts also tend to isolate, keep secrets, and lie to those close to them about their hypersexual behavior, typically experiencing debilitating shame about not just their behavior but their lies and secrecy. Sometimes they make promises to themselves and/or others that they will stop their troubling behaviors, only to find themselves right back at it just a short while later. In these respects, the challenges of sexual addiction are the same as ever. The fact that in today's world digital technology so thoroughly facilitates sexually addictive fantasies and activities is merely a byproduct of the Internet era. In other words, with sexual addiction the primary thing that has changed in recent years is the manner and speed with which addicts can locate and access the sexual content and partners that fuel their addictions.

It is also important to state that although sexnology does without doubt facilitate and drive modern-day sexual addiction, it does not appear to be a root cause of sexual addiction. In fact, as mentioned in the opening paragraph of this section, most healthy people are able to use porn, hookup apps and the like in non-compulsive and life-affirming ways. They do not become addicted, and they do not experience negative consequences. However, individuals who are pre-disposed to addiction, impulsivity, compulsivity, depression, anxiety, and the like may well struggle with sexnology, just as they might struggle with alcohol, drugs, gambling, or any other potentially addic-tive substance or activity. As such, the growing availability of digitized sexual content and partners does not increase the likelihood that these individuals will struggle in life; it merely increases the likeli-hood that their struggles will be sexual in nature.

Sex Addiction
in Women

CLAIRE, A THIRTY-TWO-YEAR-OLD real estate broker in
recovery for alcohol and cocaine addiction, is on her third
attempt at therapy. When she walks into her new therapist's office, she rather quickly announces, "I think I might
be bipolar." She then explains that every time she meets
a new man, she falls head over heels and jumps into bed
with him. But then, after no more than a few (always highly
sexual) dates, she finds herself backing away and looking
for someone else. She says, "As excited as I get right at the
start, after a few days the mere thought of him depresses
me. And it happens every time. I just run really hot and
cold with my relationships, so I think maybe I'm bipolar."
She then admits that her previous therapist told her point
blank that she was not bipolar, and that her issues might
be trauma and relationship driven, tied primarily to the
fact that her uncle molested her when she was twelve.
After further questioning, she admits to her new therapist
that she also has a history of relapse with stimulant drugs,

related to the ups and downs of her sex life. Either the guy she dates is using drugs and she follows suit, or she goes through a breakup and feels so depressed that she "picks up" as a form of self-medication. Claire also says that being molested has been "talked to death" with her previous therapists, and she's not interested in looking at that again. Instead, she wants to focus on her current relationship problems, along with her inability to stay clean and sober.

O ften, people think that sexual addiction is a male disorder, that women are not susceptible. And in truth, prior to the Internet, most self-identified sex addicts were indeed adult males.[1] However, as digital interconnectivity has brought easy access to an astounding array of intensely pleasurable sexual content and contacts, addiction and mental health professionals have seen a corresponding increase in the number *and variety* of people who self-report struggling with sexual addiction, including women.

Unfortunately, female sex addicts are often more difficult to diagnose and treat than male sex addicts. This may be due, at least in part, to Western socio-cultural attitudes about female sexuality. Whereas men who have a lot of sex are often celebrated as "studs" and "players," hypersexual women are typically denigrated as "sluts," "whores," and "nymphomaniacs." As such, male sex addicts are usually quite willing to discuss their sexual adventuring in treatment; they may even be quite proud of their sexual prowess despite the repeated and continually escalating negative consequences wrought by their sexual adventuring. Conversely, female sex addicts—even when they're having sex just as frequently, in the same ways, in similar venues, and with the same basic consequences as their male counterparts—tend to downplay their sexual involvement, instead discussing their behavior in terms of "relationships," or "dating," or "intimacy" often due to tremendous underlying shame. As such, clinicians must sometimes read between the lines, looking and listening clues in her history such as:

✓ A lengthy history of short, failed, sexually-charged romantic relationships
✓ Serial or multiple ongoing sexual and/or romantic affairs
✓ Using seduction and manipulation to avoid feelings of abandonment and isolation
✓ Equating sexual intensity with being/feeling in love
✓ A history of inappropriate, dysfunctional romantic or sexual relationships (with bosses, subordinates, married men, siblings, neighbors, etc.)
✓ A history of high-risk sexual activity (dangerous partners, public sex, anonymous sex, unprotected sex, etc.)
✓ A history of pairing increased alcohol and/or drug use with relationships
✓ A pattern of staying with and/or returning to abusive, neglectful, emotionally unavailable partners
✓ Recurrent periods of avoiding sex, sometimes while simultaneously engaging in other self-soothing escapist behaviors such as drinking, drugging, binge eating, compulsive spending, etc.
✓ Turning to prostitution as a cover for addictive sexual problems, often reenacting early-life sexual abuse
✓ A pattern of trading sex for companionship, money, shelter, gifts, alcohol or drugs, safety, or anything else
✓ A pattern of using weight gain to push away intimate partners, but then losing the weight and becoming hypersexual when slim
✓ Presenting to the world as a sexual object more than as a whole person. In essence, leading with sexuality (short skirts, no underwear, lots of cleavage, heavy makeup, etc.)

Claire, in the story above, is in many ways a prototypical female sex addict. For starters, she has a history of short but very intense and highly sexual relationships. She also tends to link her substance abuse problem with her relationship dissatisfaction. Furthermore, in therapy she is reticent to speak about her problems in terms of sex. Instead, like most hypersexual women, she talks more about her search for partnership, love and intimacy—even though her actual behavior is inconsistent with anything resembling the legitimate search for a mate. This "denial" is almost de rigueur among female sex addicts. Even when they are having sex several times a day with men (or women) met on social media, dating sites, hookup apps, and elsewhere, they tend to describe their behavior in terms of their dating life and their inability to find love rather than as a problem with hypersexual behavior.

As a result, sexual addiction in women is often identified only after a woman has entered treatment for another issue: most often an eating disorder, a substance-use disorder (alcoholism or drug addiction), depression, or some form of anxiety. These women seek help for the presenting issue, whatever that might be, and then act out in highly sexual ways during treatment, everything from dressing inappropriately, to disrupting group sessions with excessive flirting, to engaging in sexual activity. Some have full blown romantic affairs with other clients or even with staff members. Today, it's not at all unusual for a woman to "end up" in treatment for sexual addiction, after having been asked to leave another residential or group setting because of her behavior.

Put simply, women whose compulsive sexual behaviors are causing profound problems rarely walk into a therapist's office and self-identify as having an issue with sex. Instead, they tend to describe their problems as stemming from just about any other disorder they've read or heard about (being bipolar, in Claire's case), or, more generally, as some form of relationship trouble. Once again, this is likely caused at least in part by the fact that women, in comparison to men, face a much greater degree of internal and external shaming related to their sexual behaviors. As such, they are much less likely to admit to and seek direct help for such problems. In other words, a man who masturbates regularly and hooks up with anonymous sex partners three or four (or ten to twenty) times per week will usually rather easily self-identify as a sex addict if and when his sexual acting out causes negative life consequences. A woman seeking therapy, on the other hand, even though she may masturbate and have anonymous sex just as often as her male counterpart, is unlikely to self-identify as a sex addict, but will enter therapy for depression, drugs, food, and/ or "relationship" problems.

This woman is also much less likely than the man to be diagnosed in treatment as sexually addicted. The primary reasons for this are:

- ✓ Women are less likely than men to openly present a full sexual history (unless questioned in detail).
- ✓ Clinicians often struggle to overcome their culturally biased vision of women being less sexual than men.
- ✓ Many therapists feel uncomfortable asking detailed (potentially graphic) questions about sexual behavior, in part because they are typically not trained on how or when to do so. This is especially true when the therapist is male and the client is female.
- ✓ Female sex and love addicts tend to distort and minimize their problematic sexual behavior patterns by entering therapy complaining about other issues: dating and relationships, drug and alcohol relapse, self-harm, childhood abuse, etc.

Making an already difficult clinical task even more challenging is the fact that females are much more likely than males to present in addiction treatment with a history of overt childhood sexual abuse.[2]

We see this in the example with Claire. In such cases, well-meaning therapists will sometimes focus on resolving a woman's past sexual trauma, even when she may not yet have the emotional strength or social support to not "sexually act out" the feelings evoked when doing this incredibly difficult and highly distressing therapeutic work. At times, therapists can become so focused on traumatic early-life events that they forget to keep an eye on the other end of the spectrum: the client's adult behaviors with both self and others. A lot of women actually leave trauma-focused treatment because their lives are not improving, no matter how much they work on the past, because the adult manifestations of their trauma—sexually compulsive behaviors, intimacy disorders, not to mention nearly all forms of eating and exercise disorders—are not being actively and directly addressed.

When dealing with women and sexual addiction the therapeutic waters are often quite muddy, mostly because female sex addicts usually present with a laundry list of pressing "issues", both behavioral and historic. In Claire's case, her primary "other issue" is substance abuse. Essentially, it sounds as if Claire is having a lot of sex with a lot of different men without ever getting much out of these experiences beyond the initial excitement of sex and a new relationship. Furthermore, what follows the initial dating and sexuality experience appears to be a consistent pattern of frustration, distancing, despair and anxiety (until the next man comes along). And every time the romantic flame goes out, Claire does too, relapsing with drugs and/ or depression.

It is not unusual for women who've suffered early-life sexual trauma, as Claire did, to learn that being seductive can bring a sense of power and control over both their past and a present-day desired person/object. In Claire's case, she repeatedly plays out this search for sex while never allowing herself to get too close to any one man. Yet, she is equally unable to tolerate being alone for very long. This is often the case with female sex and love addicts, especially those with a history of early sexual trauma. These women long for healthy dependency, as we all do, but, unlike most people, they are also *relationship avoidant*, thanks to the painful expressions of intimacy they endured when they were young. They simply can't trust (or tolerate) another person enough to let that person fully know them. When these women do enter relationships, some tend to choose emotionally unavailable/addicted/abusive partners, while others keep their spouses—the very people who might safely and healthfully meet their emotional needs—at an emotional distance while acting out sexually with others.

Women, Pornography, and Addiction

It will probably shock no one to learn that there are significant differences in the ways that women and men think, act, and react. For starters, women tend to be more empathetic, while men are more analytic. Essentially, women often will view people, problems, and the world in general in a holistic way, whereas men tend to focus on the more specific. In the female world, emotions and interconnectivity are valued; in the male world, feelings and connections are seen as potential roadblocks. In other words, as John Gray writes, men are from Mars, women are from Venus.[3]

Unsurprisingly, this emotional dichotomy extends to the bedroom, with women and men experiencing both sexual attraction and sexual activity in very different ways. Essentially, women tend to be more interested in their *connection* to the other person, their *relationship* with the other person, whereas men are typically more interested in the other person's sexual body parts.

In truth, male sexual desire is actually pretty easy to comprehend. If a guy feels physically turned on, even a little bit, he's almost certainly

psychologically turned on as well (and vice versa). This means that
if a man has an erection, he wants sex. Female sexual desire is a bit
more complicated. Women can become physically sexually aroused
(increased blood flow in the reproductive organs) without becoming psychologically turned on even in the slightest. In other words,
a woman can be physically sexually aroused and not desire sex. It
seems that in (most) healthy females there is a cognitive disconnection between physical and psychological sexual arousal. With men,
this divide does not exist.

If you don't believe me, consider the difference between hardcore pornography, which even in today's world caters to a mostly
male audience, and romance novels and movies, which cater to a
mostly female audience. Most male-oriented erotica (hardcore porn)
is nothing more than an endless stream of body parts and sexual
acts, no kissing, no foreplay, no storyline, and no emotional intimacy.
Conversely, erotica for women often skips the sex act entirely, focusing instead on the nature and intensity of the couple's emotional
interaction and connection because *that* is the driving force in female
sexual desire.

In their book *A Billion Wicked Thoughts*, authors Ogi Ogas and
Sai Gaddam suggest a possible bio-evolutionary reason for this deep
difference in male and female sexual desire, writing:

WHEN CONTEMPLATING SEX WITH A MAN, a woman has to
consider the long term. This consideration may not even be
conscious, but rather is part of the unconscious software that has
evolved to protect women over hundreds of thousands of years.
Sex could commit a woman to a substantial, life-altering investment:
pregnancy, nursing, and more than a decade of child-raising.
These commitments require enormous time, resources, and energy.
Sex with the wrong guy could lead to many unpleasant outcomes....

A woman's sexual desire must be filtered through a careful appraisal of these potential risks.[4]

Admittedly, in today's world a woman no longer needs a man to successfully raise a child. But thousands of years of biological evolution are not so easily overcome, and this means that women still tend to be more turned on by relationships and intimate connections than by sexual body parts. Interestingly, pornographers have figured this out and they've monetized it in a very big way. Just consider, the female-arousal oriented *Fifty Shades of Grey* book trilogy that has sold more than 100 million copies worldwide, and the (awful!) movie which grossed more than $80 million on its opening three-day weekend.

Of course, "mommy porn," as *Fifty Shades* and its many copycats have been dubbed, doesn't "do it" for all women; some females enjoy highly objectified hardcore pornography just as much as most men do. These women are perfectly comfortable focusing on men's (or women's) body parts, and they are very clear in the idea that when they are online looking at pornography they are seeking a purely sexual experience and not an intimate connection.

Either way, it is clear that healthy women are taking advantage of digital technology's easy, anonymous access to porn—viewing and enjoying stories and imagery in the privacy of their home or on portable devices experiences that just a few years ago they couldn't have accessed without a great deal of potential cultural shaming. Because of this, more women than ever are finding pornography and casual hook-ups as a way to self-medicate stress, anxiety, depression, low self-esteem, unresolved early-life trauma, etc. And, as stated throughout this book, for some vulnerable individuals, regardless of gender, this behavior can escalate over time to the level of addiction, resulting, as all addictions do, in serious consequences. As such, pornography presents the same concerns for women as for men.

It's Not Just Single Women

RITA, A FORTY-FIVE-YEAR-OLD RESTAURATEUR, has been married for over twenty years. Recently, her husband learned she was having an affair, and he pushed for them to enter both individual and couples counseling. In their third couples' session, Rita reluctantly admitted that this wasn't her first affair, and that she'd had "a few others" over the course of their marriage. Her husband was shocked. He simply could not fathom that his beautiful wife would act in this very unlady-like way. Later, in an individual therapy session, Rita admitted that she'd actually cheated with hundreds of men over the years—more than she could count or remember. Her therapist suggested that she seek treatment for sexual addiction, which she did. At this point, she has been in treatment for six months, and has refrained from cheating dur-ing this time frame. She and her husband are still together, though the relationship is rocky because his trust has been absolutely shattered.

Of course, addiction and trauma are not the only reasons that a woman might cheat. Generally speaking, a woman who steps out on her spouse or partner does so for one of the following reasons:

1) **She feels underappreciated, neglected, or ignored.** Essen-tially, a woman who feels more like a housekeeper, financial provider, or nanny than a life partner and best friend is more vulnerable to finding an external situation that brings attention and appreciation for *whom she is* rather than the functions she performs.

2) **She craves nonsexual intimacy.** More so than men, women feel valued and connected to their relationship partner through nonsexual emotional interactions such as touching, kissing, cuddling, gift-giving, being remembered, and, most of all,

meaningful communication. Women who aren't getting these needs met by a primary partner may look elsewhere.

3) **She is not having sex at home.** Healthy adult women enjoy the physical act of sex as much as men do. They're not martyrs, and a sexless relationship may not be acceptable, even if the lack of sexual interaction is due to the male partner's medical or related issues. For these women, going outside the relationship for sex may be a logical, even healthy answer.

4) **She is bored and/or lonely.** Women who find themselves alone at home for long periods of time, perhaps when caring for young children or after children are grown and gone, may use sex to fill the void. Similarly, women who have spouses or partners who are absent for long periods of time related to work (military service, for example) may also use sex to fill the untenable emptiness.

5) **She has an intimacy disorder.** As discussed previously, childhood trauma and/or sexual abuse often leads women toward adult-life problems with addictive sexual behaviors. These women seek *emotional intensity* rather than *relationship intimacy*. Essentially, they use a constant stream of romantic and sexual activity to fulfill their unmet emotional needs, and also to avoid being vulnerable, genuine, and intimate with someone who could hurt them (as happened when they were young).

The fifth issue—an intimacy disorder—is the one with which we are concerned in this book. Basically, some women cheat because they are addicted to sex and/or the intensity of romance. Sadly, as with male addicts, they usually do not realize how profoundly their secretive sexual and/or romantic behaviors can affect the long-term emotional life of a trusting spouse or partner.

7

Love/Relationship Addiction

SHEILA IS A SINGLE, TWENTY-EIGHT-YEAR-OLD computer technician. She says that she dates constantly, but can't seem to find the right partner. "I'm online all the time," she says. "I have profiles on all sorts of dating and 'friend finder' websites and apps, looking for Mr. Right. I even joined JDate, although I'm not Jewish. I mean, why miss out on a great guy over something as minor as religion? And the crazy part is that whenever I actually met a guy on JDate, I fell for him right away and actually thought about converting to Judaism. In a couple of weeks, though, which is typical for me, I moved on to someone new. I just get bored before I can do anything too stupid, like changing religions. But it's always great when we first hook up." Although Sheila states on her profiles that she is looking for a long-term relationship, what she consistently ends up with are emotionally intense, oftentimes highly sexual short-term liaisons where the passion dissipates nearly as quickly as it forms.

"Every time I meet a new guy I think he's the one! I'm ready to drop everything and commit to him, but then I start to see the real person behind the nice smile and that ruins it. Why can't one of these guys be as good as he seems when we first meet?"

Healthy, intimate, romantic love is a beautiful thing. Unfortunately, love addiction—the endless, obsessive, dysfunctional search for romantic fulfillment—is not. When individuals are preoccupied to the point of obsession with falling and/or being in love, as love addicts are, they tend to behave in highly regrettable ways, just like alcoholics, drugs addicts, compulsive gamblers, compulsive spenders, sex addicts, etc. And, over time, love addicts inevitably experience the same basic consequences as all other addicts: depression, anxiety, lowered self-esteem, ruined relationships, trouble at work or in school, declining physical and/or emotional health, financial woes, loss of interest in family, friends, hobbies, and other previously enjoyable activities, etc.

For the most part, love addiction, also known as *relationship addiction* and *romance addiction*, is diagnosed using the same basic criteria as sexual addiction.[1] The three primary issues are:

✓ An ongoing preoccupation to the point of obsession with intense romantic fantasies and objectified new relationships

✓ An inability to exercise control over romantic fantasies and new relationships

✓ Negative consequences directly and/or indirectly related to out-of-control romantic fantasies, sexual behavior and serial relationships

Interestingly, love addicts are not actually seeking love. What they're really chasing, over and over and over, is the emotional escape provided by the rush of first romance, sometimes referred to as *limerence*. Limerence is the psychological term for the initial stage of a romantic relationship, when intensity and infatuation rule the day. Limerence is when the heart races because you're together and aches when you're apart. It's that brief period when literally everything about the other person seems fascinating and exciting—even the stuff that will eventually become annoying seems "just so cute," at the start. During the limerence stage of a romantic relationship, potential problems are easily overridden by the excitement and the intensity of meeting someone new and attractive and funny and interesting who just might be "the one." But as they are unknown, the potential object of the addict's affection remains just that—an object—and not a real person.

Limerence, like other pleasure responses, is caused by a neurochemical surge, primarily the release of dopamine, along with oxytocin, adrenaline, serotonin, and various other pleasure-related endorphins. As you may recall from discussions in Chapters 1 and 3, this is the same basic (emotionally escapist) neurobiological reaction evoked by addictive substances like cocaine and heroin, and addictive behaviors like compulsive sex, compulsive gambling, compulsive spending, and the like. So is it any wonder that people sometimes get hooked on the escapist high of early romance?

This does not mean that limerence is a bad thing. In fact, generally speaking, limerence is a good thing, as it keeps couples together long enough to find out if they might have something beyond just an initial attraction. As such, limerence is an evolutionary imperative—the glue that keeps new couples attached until the desire to build a life together (including having and raising kids) kicks in, or until they intelligently realize that they're not right for each other and decide to move on.

In truth, almost everyone can identify with this early, thoroughly fixated relationship stage in which the other person's daily activities and very existence become an obsessive source of emotional excitement and distraction. Of course, most people are not love addicted, and, as such, they innately understand that healthy romantic relationships evolve over time into somewhat less immediately exciting, but ultimately more meaningful long-term intimacy. In other words, emotionally healthy people understand that the initial rush of romance (limerence) is a stage, a temporary state, rather than the end product of an intimate relationship. Love addicts, however, seek to perpetually extend this emotional high using it to lose themselves in the same way (and for the same reasons) that substance abusers, compulsive gamblers, sex addicts, and other addicts abuse their substance or behavior of choice.

What love addicts fail to understand is that *limerence is not the same as long-term intimacy.* Love addicts choose to live in limerence, relying on this neurochemical rush as their primary way to avoid feeling stress and other forms of emotional discomfort. In other words, love addicts use the naturally occurring high of limerence for escape and dissociation, just as alcoholics, drug addicts, sex addicts, compulsive gamblers, and such use the neurochemical high of addictive substances and/or behaviors to numb out and not experience the ups and downs of life.

Love addicts spend the bulk of their time either searching for the perfect love interest or wriggling out of their current relationship so they can focus on a new one. They constantly check their profiles on Match.com, eHarmony, Ashley Madison (even though they're not married), JDate (even though they're not Jewish), etc. Almost every decision they make—what to wear, where to eat, where to socialize, where to exercise, what job to have—is colored by their desire to meet and hook their perfect partner, the one person who can make them feel complete and whole and perpetually excited about their relationship.

Behavior patterns commonly exhibited by love addicts of both genders include the following:

- ✓ Relying on romantic fantasy as a way to escape from stress and other types of emotional discomfort
- ✓ Mistaking short term sexual and/or romantic intensity for love and genuine, lasting intimacy
- ✓ Constantly struggling to maintain the sexual/romantic intensity of an existing relationship, thus creating unnecessary drama—yet often feeling stuck and trapped when in one
- ✓ Feeling desperate and alone when not in a relationship
- ✓ Using sex, seduction and manipulation to hook or hold on to a partner
- ✓ After a failed relationship, using anonymous sex, porn, and/or compulsive masturbation to avoid "needing" someone
- ✓ Promising over and over to give up on relationships and focus on self-care, only to swiftly be back out there looking for companionship
- ✓ Giving up important personal interests, beliefs, and/or friendships to maximize time in a romantic relationship or to please a romantic partner
- ✓ Missing out on important commitments (with family, work, or elsewhere) to search for a new relationship or to fix an existing relationship
- ✓ Seeking a new relationship while still in a relationship
- ✓ Feigning interest in activities you don't enjoy as a way meet someone new or to keep an existing partner

✓ Consistently choosing partners who are emotionally unavailable, addicted, verbally abusive, and/or physically abusive [2]

Sadly, romance addicts typically think they're searching for real, lasting love. In reality, however, they're perpetually chasing the excitement of new romance without any real understanding of the fact that this early relationship stage is fleeting and not indicative of healthy, mature, lasting intimacy. Love addicts repeatedly chase the "rush" they experience when they meet someone new, sometimes discarding many perfectly good potential long-term partners along the way simply because the intensity of the romance has waned. (For a detailed explanation of the neurobiological difference between limerence and love, see Chapter 17.)

Love/Relationship Addiction
Versus Sexual Addiction

Love addicts abuse objectified romantic fantasy and the accompanying intense neurochemical rush caused when falling "deeply in love" to achieve the same type of escapist emotional self-stabilization as sex addicts do, and, as such, they are usually just as detached from the reality of their situation. The primary difference between sex addicts and love addicts is that sex addicts tend to direct their attention toward whomever or whatever is in the vicinity, often chasing multiple "fixes" (anonymous sex, casual sex, affairs, porn, etc.) over a relatively short period, whereas love addicts tend to focus obsessively on having, finding or keeping "the person" or "the relationship." Typically, this one person becomes the sole object of the love addict's life. Recreation, friends, work, and other interests fall by the wayside.

Love addicts sometimes *look* and *act* quite a bit like sex addicts, that is, engaging in lots of sex with lots of people. However, love addicts use sex as a tool for hooking and/or holding on to a romantic partner, whereas sex addicts typically do the opposite, using the lure of romance to obtain a sexual partner. In short, love addicts are chasing escape and dissociation via romantic fantasy and activity, while sex addicts are chasing escape and dissociation via sexual fantasy and activity.

Love addicts, like sex addicts, are largely in denial about the problematic nature of what they are doing. Rather than recognizing that *they are the common denominator* in their endless failed relationships, love addicts typically place the blame on their dates, lovers, partners, spouses, and anyone else with whom they've ever become entangled. Sometimes they become intensely controlling and demanding, trying to get their objectified partner to love them the way they want to be loved, regardless of whether the other person is actually capable or interested in doing that. Then, when that person inevitably fails them, they act out romantically once again, beginning anew their obsessive search for "the right one." Over time, their willful blindness to personal experience traps them in a downwardly spiraling cycle of behaviors that both causes and increases their unhappiness.

Sexual Orientation and Sex Addiction

As I have stated repeatedly throughout this book, sexual addiction has nothing whatsoever to do with who or what turns a person on. Instead, it is based on the same three factors as every other form of addiction:

1) Ongoing obsession/preoccupation with the drug/ behavior of choice
2) Loss of control over use
3) Directly related negative life consequences

This means that gay and lesbian sex addicts are not compulsively sexual because of their sexual orientation. Rather, they are compulsively sexual as a way to self-soothe stress, emotional discomfort, and the pain of underlying psychological issues like anxiety, depression, low self-esteem, shame, attachment deficits, unresolved childhood and/or severe-adult trauma, etc. In this respect, gay and lesbian sex addicts are exactly like heterosexual sex addicts. They are also exactly like gambling addicts, alcoholics, drug addicts, compulsive spenders, and the like. However, as with any repressed minority culture, there are differences that do require some investigation here.

Gay Men and Promiscuity

There is a widely held misperception that all gay men are, by nature, compulsively sexual. And in truth, gay male Western culture has traditionally held fewer formal and defined "rules" about monogamy then, let's say, any average heterosexual married couple. But the reasons have more to do with the fact that it is men seeking out men for sex, rather than the fact that gay men are simply promiscuous (not true). It is true that if you are a man looking to have sex with a man in our culture it is easier to find a partner than if you are looking for a woman. The reasons may seem obvious (more about healthy female sexuality versus healthy male sexuality in a later chapter), but the simple fact is that most men are more willing (due to the way we are built psychologically) to have objectified, non-relational sexual experiences than are most women. Many men are "ready to go" for sex with the right person if they look hot, the time is available, and they both want to make it happen. Healthy women seeking sex tend to look not only for hot bodies but also for an emotional connection to that person (or at least a perceived emotional connection), before being sexual. That might mean dinner and a movie before having sex, all of which takes time, but finding a man for sex often doesn't always mean having to emotionally connect to him to "get some."

Anonymous sex doesn't involve getting to know someone, taking them to dinner, meeting before sex; sometimes words are not even exchanged. This is not a typical scenario that most women would join—and good for them because women are clearly more at risk in a variety of ways in these kinds of sexual encounters. Many men are okay with no dinner, no meet and greet, no love, no flowers or candy—just the sex, thank you very much. The bottom line is that it is more difficult and takes more time for straight men to find a woman for casual sex (unless they are paying for it—think strip clubs, adult clubs, etc). Whereas gay men seeking out other men for causal sex have more opportunity to "get some" than do their straight brethren.

In days of yore (a mere ten or fifteen years ago), men who were interested in being sexual with other men searched for sex in bars, in adult bookstores and theaters, in sex clubs and bathhouses, in the steam room at their local gym, in public parks and restrooms, and on notorious street corners late at night. These choices were adaptive ways of finding men with similar needs and desires in a culture of profound cultural repression, but none of these sex-seeking venues were ideal. And sometimes they were downright dangerous. In fact, many older gay men vividly remember the days when gay cruising spots were routinely raided by police, with denizens hauled off in paddy wagons and jailed for the night—with their names and "crimes" published in the next morning's paper. This was actually commonplace from the 1950s through the 1970s, and even into the 1980s in some locales. And because many people's exposure to homosexuals (and homosexuality) was limited to newspaper narrations of the local police blotter, the common perception of gay and bisexual men was understandably skewed toward the "sex-crazed" label.

Happily, this is changing. Homosexuality is no longer illegal or looked upon by the mental health community as pathological. Gay and lesbian community today seek sex in much safer (i.e., less public) venues, primarily through online dating and hookup websites and apps like Adam4Adam, Grindr, Bear411, Manhunt, Dattch, Pink-Cupid, and the like. Today, even mainstream dating sites like *Match.com* have specialized sections for gay and bisexual men and women. And marriage, rather than "getting laid," is increasingly the "go to" goal for many young gay men.

Nevertheless, living in a counterculture in which unfettered sexual activity is expected and even celebrated can enable compulsive sexual behaviors. This relatively open expectation/celebration of "alternative sexuality" (i.e., "no one is going to tell me how to live my sex life!") is in many ways a natural and healthy reaction to the ubiquitous ongoing repression and abuse of gay and lesbian men and women. On the plus side, this assertive response to living in a shame-based, homophobic culture has helped many gays and lesbians to "come out" and live honestly, developing healthy intimate relationships with the partner(s) of their choice. On the other hand, this tacit community approval of unrestrained sexual expression has enabled the sexual addictions of countless gay and lesbian people.

Consider alcohol as an analogy for this. An alcoholic who spends all of his free time in bars will likely find it very easy to rationalize, minimize, and justify (to deny) his drinking problem since everyone else around him is also drinking. Thus the gay sex addict who is hanging out in sex focused venues (online or real world) where everyone else is also being highly sexual (gay bars, bathhouses, Grindr, porn sites, etc.), has a background against which he can or she can rationalize, minimize, and justify the sex that he or she is having—even if his or her sexual behaviors spiral out of control.

Lesbian Women, Sex, and Love Addiction

Sadly, there is little to no research on lesbian women who sexually act out in addictive and compulsive ways. This doesn't mean there isn't such a population; certainly there are lesbians who go from bar to bar and woman to woman, using these people more as objects than as lovers and partners. But, in fact, fewer lesbian women present for sexual addiction treatment than do straight women (more on women and sex addiction in chapters to come).

The challenge for intimacy disordered lesbians, women who have endured the kinds of early abuse, trauma, and neglect referenced in the chapter, "why me," seems to show up more as a problematic pattern of intimacy or relationship-disordered behaviors (discussed in later love/relationship chapters). In these cases, most typically a gay woman (often feeling desperately lonely when single, and struggling to simply enjoy her time when single) will very quickly "fall in love" with another attractive woman, often having sex right away with great intensity—but also seeking to live with this woman and/or get very close very quickly (often without enough time to fully know each other). In these situations she will repeatedly find herself distancing herself over time (on many levels), from the very person who was so fascinating to her just a few months before. Some will distance emotionally with walls and silence, some sexually, others by gaining a great deal of weight and thus literally creating a physical barrier to sex and intimacy. When single, this woman will then often lose the weight and go back out on "the hunt" for a new spouse. This pattern of "serial monogamy" seems to fit many intimacy challenged women in general and lesbians in particular.

The first book to scientifically examine this pattern is very recent and is called *The Urge to Merge* by Lauren Costine, PhD. Dr. Costine discusses this issue at length and it is well worth a read for lesbian women concerned that they may be struggling with an intimacy disorder.

Recognizing and Dealing with
Internalized Homophobia

For many gay and lesbian sex addicts, negative self-beliefs are an integral component of the addictive process, helping to support a shame-based sense of self. These negative self-hating views often manifest as internalized homophobia, which is nearly always magnified and intensified by social and familial nonacceptance and nonsupport. Then, if addictive patterns of same-sex sexuality enter the picture, preexisting shame and self-hatred are compounded, with the only relief being a temporary escape through still more addictive sex. This is the crux of the sexually addictive cycle for many gays and lesbians: layering shame upon shame and perpetually reinforcing an already badly distorted self-image.

Knowing this, it is unsurprising that some gay and lesbian sex addicts also present in treatment with *ego-dystonic* (i.e., self-loathing) feelings related to their sexual orientation. In other words, they desperately wish that they were not attracted to members of the same sex. Ultimately these addicts must be treated for their negative feelings related to their sexual orientation, as well as their problematic patterns of sexual acting out. That said, containment of addictive sexual behaviors should always be the initial intervention and treatment focus.

Under no circumstances should a therapist, counselor or clergy member ever try to alter a client's sexual orientation or make such promises by calling it "sex addiction." Sexual orientation is fixed and immutable. In other words, gay men are sexually and romantically attracted to other men, lesbians are sexually and romantically attracted to other women, bisexuals are sexually and romantically attracted to both genders, and heterosexuals are attracted to the opposite sex—and no amount of aversion therapy, talk therapy, social pressure, or prayer is going to change that.[1] Thus understandably, "gay conversion therapy" just plain does not work. Certainly a person can choose to not act on his or her same-sex attractions, but that doesn't make those attractions go away. The American Psychiatric Association states this rather clearly, writing:

[PEOPLE] CANNOT CHOOSE TO BE EITHER GAY OR STRAIGHT. For most people, sexual orientation emerges in early adolescence without any prior sexual experience. Although we can choose whether to act on our feelings, psychologists do not consider sexual orientation to be a conscious choice that can be voluntarily changed.[2]

Sadly, in addition to being a waste of time and money, attempts to change a person's sexual orientation are actually quite harmful, especially to young people (some of whom are involuntarily subjected to these "treatments"). For the most part, this damage is caused by gay conversion therapy's reinforcement of societal prejudices against homosexuality. In one study looking at the effects of social and familial rejection on gay and lesbian youth, researchers found that gay and lesbian kids who experience significant feelings of rejection because of their sexual orientation—such as what occurs with gay conversion therapy—are three times as likely to use illicit drugs, six times as likely to report high levels of depression, and eight times as likely to attempt suicide.[3] Recognizing these dangers, two states, California and New Jersey, have passed laws outlawing the practice of so called "gay conversion" therapy on minors, while virtually every major medical and psychotherapeutic professional organization has issued a statement condemning it.

Sex and Drug Abuse Combined

As discussed in detail in Chapter 8, cross and co-occurring addictions are quite common among sex addicts. And given that gay and lesbian men and women generally have higher rates of addiction across the board,[4] it is reasonable to assume that the rates of sexual addiction might also be higher. One study found that 69 percent of heterosexual male sex addicts versus 80 percent of homosexual male sex addicts admitted to a cross or co-occurring addiction or some other similarly problematic behavior.[5] Further, as with sex addicts in general, stimulant drugs like cocaine and methamphetamine seem most often to be the co-occurring drug of choice. And when that is the case, the two addictions often fuse, becoming so tightly paired that engaging in one behavior inevitably leads to the other. And, as mentioned later in this book, this is double trouble in terms of both potential consequences and risk for relapse, making the healing process that much more challenging to achieve.

Note: Some gay men reading this chapter may identify with it or question it in ways that require a deeper look at gay men and sex addiction versus gay men and healthy sexuality. This author's 2013 book, *Cruise Control: Understanding Sex Addiction in Gay Men*, is fully dedicated to helping gay and bisexual men who wish to learn more about sex addiction and can be readily found both online and in stores. As stated in the text, lesbian women seeking more information on sex and intimacy disorders are encouraged to read Dr. Lauren Costine's *The Urge to Merge*, which is also widely available and dedicated to gay women with similar questions about themselves and their relationships.

9

When Sex Pairs with Other Addictions

S exual addiction is often not a stand-alone issue. In fact, a significant percentage of sex addicts also deal with *cross* and/or *co-occurring* addictions.[1] Individuals who are cross-addicted switch from one addiction to another, whereas people with co-occurring addictions deal with multiple addictions simultaneously. Typically, cross and co-addicted people move seamlessly from one substance to another, from one behavior to another, and even from substances to behaviors and behaviors to substances. Examples of cross-addiction include the following:

> Dan, a married father of two, alternates between periods of sexting and having webcam sex with women he's met on one or more hookup apps and binge drinking. He acts out sexually until he feels so ashamed that he decides to stop, and then he starts drinking.

He continues with the drinking until he feels so ashamed that he decides to stop, and then he starts to act out sexually. He continually switches from one addiction to the other.

After leaving treatment for sex and love addiction, Alice, who had never struggled with her weight while active in her sex and love addiction, gained 40 pounds in less than a year, replacing her intensely focused sexual and romantic acting out with another addiction: binge eating.

Examples of co-occurring addictions include the following:

Jane began drinking in her early teens, after she was sexually abused by a family member. Shortly thereafter, she began dating. On dates, she struggled with her adolescent desire to explore her sexuality, so she drank to numb those feelings. Over time, drinking and sexual activity became one and the same. When she drank, she wanted sex. When she didn't drink, she avoided sex altogether. Now in her late thirties, she can't stop drinking, nor can she stop being sexual.

Evan, a young gay man, loves the feeling of sex when he's high on crystal meth. Every night after work, he activates his Grindr profile and does a few "bumps." After a hit or two of meth, all he cares about is sex—and the more the merrier. Sometimes he hooks up with five or six guys in a single night. Most of the time he takes Viagra with the meth because he can't maintain an erection without assistance. Then, when the evening finally winds down, he drinks an entire bottle of cough syrup to put himself to sleep.

As mentioned above, cross and co-occurring addictions are relatively common with sex addicts. One survey of 1,603 self-identified sex addicts found that 69 percent of heterosexual men, 79 percent of heterosexual women, and 80 percent of homosexual men admitted to a cross or co-occurring addiction, or some other similarly problematic behavior.[2] Another survey of self-identified sex addicts found that 58 percent reported either current or past issues with drug addiction, and 31 percent reported either current or past issues with alcoholism. Compulsive gambling (29 percent), compulsive video gaming (37 percent), eating disorders (47 percent), and compulsive spending (49 percent) were also common.[3]

Below are some of the many ways that addicts can shift their obsession from one substance or experience to another:[4]

1) **Alternating Cycles:** switching back and forth from one addiction to another, often for years on end (i.e., flipping between binge-drinking and sexual acting out)

2) **Combining:** when various addictive substances/behaviors are combined to create the perfect high (i.e., mixing meth with porn and then cybersex)

3) **Cross-Tolerance:** using one addiction as a way to tolerate another (i.e., getting drunk to self-soothe shame about sexual behaviors)

4) **Disinhibiting:** using one addiction to reduce inhibitions related to a second addiction (i.e., getting high before having sex with a stranger)

5) **Fusing:** using one addiction to amplify another (i.e., using cocaine to heighten the pleasure of orgasm)

6) **Inhibiting:** viewing one addiction as the lesser of two evils (i.e., smoking cigarettes instead of looking at porn all night)

7) **Masking:** using one addiction to hide another (i.e., going to AA for alcoholism but never looking at compulsive sexual activity)

8) **Numbing:** using one addiction to numb the shame of another (i.e., getting drunk after cheating on your spouse)

9) **Replacement:** replacing one addiction with another (i.e., cutting down on the use of hookup apps by gambling for hours on end)

10) **Rituals:** incorporating one addiction into the ritual phase of another (i.e., buying meth before beginning the search for a prostitute)

11) **Withdrawal Mediation:** using one addiction to stop another (i.e., shopping compulsively as a way to stay out of sex clubs)

Stimulants and Sex Addiction

With sex addicts, stimulant drugs like cocaine and methamphetamine (aka, "meth" or "crystal meth") are often the co-occurring drug of choice. Alcohol, GHB, MDMA, and various other "party drugs" are also used in conjunction with sexual addiction, but cocaine and meth are most prevalent. This is because cocaine and meth allow users to be sexual for several hours (or even days) at a time, especially when erection enhancers like Viagra, Levitra, and/or Cialis are along for the ride. On hookup websites and apps, cocaine and meth are often used as an inducement for sex, with profiles saying things like, "Come over and party with me and my BFF Crystal." A more simple tactic is simply stating that one is looking to PNP, with "PNP" standing for "party and play." It is well understood in the digital hookup community that the "party" portion of the adventure will involve a stimulant like cocaine or meth, perhaps commingled with porn, multiple sex partners, and days-on-end sexual encounters.

Unfortunately, stimulant drugs are highly disinhibiting, which means the user's beliefs about the need for safer sex will often disappear when high, greatly increasing the risk for HIV and other

STDs, unwanted pregnancies, etc. Furthermore, stimulant abuse is highly destructive in its own right, both physically and mentally. Exacerbating matters is the fact that many men and women with a co-occurring sex and stimulant addiction also abuse alcohol, benzodiazepines (Valium, Ativan, Xanax, etc.), and/or over-the-counter cold medicines as a way to "come down" and get some sleep when the party is finally over.

When stimulant drug abuse is consistently fused with the hunt for and experience of intensely arousing sex, these paired behavioral patterns can become mutually reinforcing. Over time, even simple sexual fantasies and/or memories of past sexual acts can become a psychological trigger to abuse drugs, and vice versa. Eventually, without help, stimulant drug use and sexual activity can become so tightly paired that engaging in one behavior inevitably leads to the other. For this type of dually addicted individual, getting high and seeking/finding/having sex becomes a single coexisting and complementary addiction.

A study focusing on gay men who struggle with meth abuse strongly supports the idea that stimulant abuse and sexual activity can become so intertwined that drugs and sex are no longer separate addictions.[5] In fact, the study found that for some gay men the leading reason for meth use was "sexual enhancement," with test subjects stating that meth use both lowered their sexual inhibitions and prolonged the duration of their sexual acting out. Other research has provided similar findings, with one study of heterosexual male and female meth users finding that males typically cited a "desire to boost sexual pleasure" as a primary reason for using.[6] Yet another study found that meth use increases the likelihood of numerous high-risk sexual behaviors, and that binge drug use in particular is strongly associated with binge sexual activity, an increased number of sexual partners, and unprotected sex.[7]

Among clinicians who routinely treat sex addicts (and also stimulant drug abusers), the studies cited above are probably not surprising. The most important thing to note here is that when drug and sex addictions intertwine and fuse in this way, treatment and recovery become much more difficult. In short, the dual addiction to stimulants and sex is double trouble in terms of both potential consequences and risk for relapse. Usually, these dual addicts must be treated for both of their addictions simultaneously. Otherwise, they are unlikely to heal from either.

Co-Occurring Addictions: Where to Start?

If you struggle with both substance and behavioral addictions— for example alcohol and sex or drugs and spending, etc.—there is a general treatment rule of thumb, which applies here. Unless there is a profound safety or relationship component that applies to your sexual behavior (i.e., a spouse about to leave you, you are having unsafe sex, you are going to get arrested where you go see prostitutes, etc.), *then get sober FIRST from drugs and alcohol.* As mentioned previously in this book, alcohol and other substances are by nature disinhibiting, meaning that there are things you would not do or say sober that you may well do or say when loaded. This may be true of your problem sexual and romantic patterns. It may well be that when you stop using, the problem sex stops, too. If that is the case you likely do not have concurrent addictions (substances and sex), but rather your drinking and using leads you to sexual behavior you don't feel good about or want to do sober. Better to take care of your using first and then see what sexual issues remain.

Many addicts who are truly dually addicted (substances and behaviors) will not able to address a behavioral issue (sex, gaming, gambling, etc.) while still getting high. And the reality is that it is very hard to stay focused on sexual and romantic behaviors when trudging through the challenges of early drug and alcohol sobriety. For this person, it may also be best to first get sober on drugs/alcohol and then start reigning in and working on sex/relationship issues.

Some addicts don't have the luxury of choosing which addiction to work on first (substances or behaviors), due to the immediacy of their life situation and/or addiction-related consequences. For such people (double-dippers as they are known in the recovery community), there is a need to get sober simultaneously *from both substances and behaviors*. In these cases, it takes a tremendous amount of work and support—daily meetings, multiple support groups, therapies and even sponsors, etc.—to get there. Trying to get sober on more than one addiction at a time is a big task. Therefore, it is not unusual for such people to enter residential treatment in order to have a safe place to deal with both issues simultaneously, or at least get sober on substances first, with life's stressors left behind while doing so. If you are among these folks, and you go away to get help, you will find yourself welcomes and well-supported in treatment, a process can often provide life-changing experiences over as few as twenty-eight to thirty-five days. Getting sober while in working in a holistic rehab/trauma program can be much like a year of therapy in a month as well-designed and well-run treatment centers can and do change lives for the good, every day.

Why Do So Many (Sex) Addicts Have Cross and/or Co-Occurring Addictions?

Sex addicts aren't the only addicts prone to cross and co-occurring addictions. The simple fact is that whatever the addiction—sex, drugs, alcohol, gambling, eating, or anything else—the motivation is the same. The addict wants to feel better, which actually means the addict wants to feel *less* (i.e., to control what he or she is feeling). As discussed throughout this book, addictive substances and behaviors all happily oblige by altering brain chemistry in ways that temporarily distract the individual from stress, emotional discomfort, and the pain of underlying psychological conditions like depression, anxiety, attachment deficit disorders, unresolved early-life or severe adult trauma, etc.

Certainly some addicts are purists, sticking with their drug or behavior of choice no matter what. For others, however, their primary addiction is just one part of a larger pattern. These individuals are sometimes referred to as "garbage can users," ingesting whatever addictive substance or engaging in whatever addictive behavior is available, as long as it creates the escapist neurochemical rush they seek.

Ultimately, whatever the addiction, the result is always the same:

- ✓ A compelling craving for the substance/behavior
- ✓ A negative impact on health, self-esteem, family, relationships, finances, career, etc.
- ✓ An inability to stop using the substance/behavior despite adverse consequences

Sadly, as mentioned above, for some sex addicts co-occurring addictions can become inextricably linked. This means that if the addict is engaging in one activity, he or she is almost certainly engaging in the other. In such cases, the addict must address both of his or her addictions simultaneously. Otherwise, he or she may not recover from either.

Mental Health and Sexual Addiction

Some sex and relationship addicts also describe liefelong challenges with emotional and mental health problems like: mood disorders (depression, anxiety), profound social problems, ADD, OCD, bipolar disorder and schizophrenia. While some people in early sexual recovery do report that previously strong symptoms of depression, anxiety—even paranoia—were lifted from them when they got sexually sober, this may not be true for everyone. The hope and optimism comes out of telling your sexual secrets, releasing your sexual shame, and being offered a path toward healing is powerful and life changing. However, your mental health is nothing to take lightly and addiction may well be the least of your problems, at the start. If you have been diagnosed with a mental health problem (other than addiction), one that is not quickly alleviated by a commitment to sexual behavior change and related supportive therapy, then those issues will have to be managed alongside your sexual behavior problems and/or before you start the sexual recovery process. No one who is actively untreated, unmedicated, and feeling out of control with depression, anxiety, isolation, sleeplessness, hearing voices, etc., will be able to fully bring sexual addiction into remission until they take on their mental health problems and get the help needed to heal. There are resources at every level for people to gain mental health. If you need to access yours, do so without hesitation for it is key to your healing.

Note, too, that there are certain mental health concerns—specifically ADD, OCD, and the manic phase of bi-polar disorder, where hypersexual behavior can appear as part of these diagnoses. If you have one of these disorders getting onto and staying on medication, while fully attending to your mental health, may be the answer to your sexual acting out. If not, you will again have to attend to both issues fully in order to heal.

10

How to Get Better

JEREMY IS A SINGLE, THIRTY-NINE-YEAR-OLD police officer, now in recovery for sexual addiction. For years he put instant sexual gratification ahead of everything except work—even though he wasn't having much actual sex. Instead, when not working, he would "find himself" abusing porn, masturbating on webcam, or playing virtual sex games on his laptop. Nevertheless, he wanted a true relationship, and he occasionally tried to date in real life, but without success. "When I was on dates, all I was really thinking about was going home and getting off. Even if a date ended in sex, I would rush home afterward and masturbate to porn." Over the years, Jeremy grew lonely, isolated, and depressed. He went to multiple therapists to work on his depression, and at one point feeling utterly alone, hopeless, and ashamed of himself he even considered ending his life. Finally, in desperation he found a therapist who knew about sexual addiction, asked in detail about his sexual life, and thus identified his primary problem. Working with this therapist, Jeremy crafted a plan for change and healing. Today he is sexually sober for fifteen months and his depression has lifted. He says that despite his past, he now feels hopeful for the first time in many years about himself, his life, and his sense of being a good man. On the advice of his therapist and friends in recovery, he has not yet started dating, but he feels increasingly ready to begin that process and is preparing guidelines with his therapist to begin doing just that.

Getting Started

Like any addict who is mired in a problem of his own making, when a sex addict is ready to heal, he or she will nearly always require outside support and assistance. After all, if they could change their behaviors on their own (without help), they would do so, but they cannot. And this is not surprising when you understand the factors that drive the problem: primarily an unbroken cycle of triggers, acting out, and denial, plus a big dollop of lies, secrecy, shame, and self-loathing. To overcome these dynamics, addicts nearly always need the insight and the accountability that only an objective outsider can provide. In short, shame and remorse about compulsive sexual behaviors and even the worst related consequences are not enough to keep a sex addict from backsliding when challenged by emotional and/or psychological discomfort. Without external support, willpower alone just doesn't seem enough, and sex addicts' endless promises to change—made to themselves and others—almost inevitably fall by the wayside at some point.

The good news is that with proper guidance and support, lasting behavior change and a healthier life are absolutely possible. Before beginning this journey toward emotional healing and sexual recovery, it is important that sex addicts understand they will need to keep an open mind and become honest about their sexual thoughts and behaviors. This is never easy, of course, but it is always well worth the effort, as long-term healing from sexual addiction can foster a rediscovery of self and a much more rewarding creative and connected life.

If sex addicts are married or in an otherwise committed relationship and a committed partner (despite their anger and hurt) is open to staying around and joining in the healing process, couple's recovery can bring a deeper understanding of both their own and their partner's emotional needs and desires, while encouraging and allowing both parties to become more emotionally intimate with each other. If sex addicts are not in a romantic relationship, recovery builds self-esteem and enables them to make healthier choices about dating, sexuality, and (if they so desire) the formation of a long-term intimate partnership.

As sex addicts heal from active addiction, honesty, integrity, self-knowledge, and a desire to be vulnerable and known for who they truly are, warts and all, slowly but steadily replaces the double life they've been living. Secrets, lies, and superficial connections fall away, as they begin to feel better about their behavior and their self-identity. When taken on actively and honestly, sexual recovery can bring about unexpected levels of emotional maturity and hope for a future filled with loving, life-affirming friendships and romantic relationships. Admittedly, working toward change is not easy, especially when dealing with a deeply rooted addiction, and/or a betrayed spouse, but it pays big dividends over time.

Initial Steps Toward Healing

Interestingly, even though sex addicts nearly always require outside assistance if they hope to heal, the first step on their healing journey is an internal one: deciding that they actually want help with their addiction. Typically, this willingness to enter into the often difficult process of recovery arises because the addict has experienced negative consequences related to his or her sexual behaviors. Often the addict's marriage or primary relationship, job, standing in the community, or freedom is threatened. Sometimes motivation is also internal, with the addict simply not liking the person that he or she has become and wanting to change. It doesn't really matter where the initial impetus comes from—even superficial remorse (the desire to not get in any-more trouble), can get the ball rolling—as long as there is genuine motivation for change.

Once a sex addict is motivated to change and willing to accept outside assistance, it's time to get to work. This process starts with finding an accountability partner. An accountability partner is a person who holds the addict accountable for the work that must be done, often providing feedback as it happens. This supportive guide is typically a therapist, a twelve-step sexual recovery sponsor, a non-shaming clergy member, or a close friend who is also healing from sexual addiction. (For addicts not yet willing or ready to seek in-person assistance, certain websites and twelve-step groups offer online and/or phone support.* But it is best to seek face-to-face help if/when available.) *It is not advised for sex addicts to use a spouse or any other romantic partner as their accountability partner* because those individuals are nearly always too close to the situation—and often too injured by the situation—to provide the objective input that is needed. This is true even when a spouse wishes to help.

Ultimately, the job of an accountability partner is to assist and guide the sex addict—in person, by phone, or even online—with identifying what his or her recovery-related commitments and pri-orities actually are, and ways in which those commitments toward change can be met and maintained. Accountability partners are also

---

* See resources section for more details.

there for support when sex addicts experience moments of weakness. As such, establishing and developing this connection is an essential element of growing and maintaining sexual recovery and healing.

A few of the more common and highly useful early-recovery commitments that an accountability partner might ask a sex addict to make include the following:**

- ✓ Promise to reach out immediately if you feel triggered to act out sexually. (Feeling triggered is inevitable, and there is nothing wrong with it, so long as addicts start dealing with their triggers in a healthy, nonaddictive way and not acting out their triggers.)
- ✓ Promise to reach out immediately if you actually do act out sexually. (Slips and relapse are common in early recovery from sexual addiction.) They must be honestly admitted and gleaned for insight.
- ✓ Throw away all physical material related to the problem. (For instance, porn addicts need to throw out all books, magazines, VHS tapes, DVDs, flash drives, and other storage devices that contain pornographic imagery or stories, along with any related paraphernalia such as lubricants and sex toys. It is best to throw this material into a commercial Dumpster at least a mile from home. Sometimes accountability partners will supervise this process to make sure the addict does not enjoy the material one last time.)
- ✓ Go through your computer, laptop, tablet, smartphone, etc., deleting any and all files, emails, texts, sexts, bookmarks, profiles, apps, and contact information related to your addiction. Use the search capabilities built into your digital devices to

---

** These tasks are often required with or without the use of an accountability partner.

look for these items. In other words, search for .gif, .tif, .jpeg, .wmv, .mpg, .mpeg, .mp4, .avi, and .mov files, among others. If possible, and if it won't disrupt other areas of your life, disable the webcams on these devices. (Again, accountability partners often supervise this process to make sure the addict does not "enjoy the material just one last time.")

✓ Cancel any sex addiction-related memberships to websites, apps, and/or bricks-and-mortar establishments, along with any credit cards you've used to pay for these memberships to make sure they don't automatically renew. (If addicts don't want to cancel these cards, they can call the credit card company and report the card as lost. Credit card companies will gladly send replacement cards with different numbers, and this serves the same purpose as cancellation.)

✓ Commit that you will stay away from "gray area" activities. (In the same way that alcoholics new to recovery should not hang out in bars, sex addicts shouldn't leave the Victoria's Secret catalog on the coffee table, frequent NC-17 movies, or get massages from strangers. People who are not sexually addicted can handle these things without becoming triggered; sex addicts cannot. So it is best to stay away from them.)

✓ Commit to only using digital devices where others can see you. At work and at home, orient computers and other digital devices so the screens are publicly visible. With portable digital devices, use them only in public places when others are around. (Recovering sex addicts need to understand that using these devices in private, even for a legitimate nonsexual purpose, is a gray area activity that could easily trigger the desire to act out.)

✓ Create reminders of why you want to change your behavior. Use pictures of your spouse or kids as background imagery on your digital devices. Use your wedding song or your spouse's voice as your ringtone, etc. (Visual and auditory reminders of what sex addicts stand to lose can be powerful motivation for change.)

✓ Purchase and install "parental control software." (These filtering, blocking, tracking, and accountability software products prevent access to problematic online venues and monitor a person's overall use of digital devices, typically providing reports to an accountability partner. See the Resources chapter for more information on these products.)

✓ Create and implement a plan for sexual sobriety. (This plan is best developed working in conjunction with the accountability partner. It will likely take the form of a sexual boundary plan. Sexual boundary plans are discussed at length as this chapter progresses.)

Sexual Sobriety Versus Sexual Abstinence

Sexual addicts in the early stages of recovery and healing typically have little to no idea what the term "sexual sobriety" actually means. Many worry that sexual sobriety mirrors chemical sobriety, where permanent abstinence from all mood altering substances is required. In fact, sex addicts new to treatment often pose some form of the following question: "Will I still get to have a regular sex life?" or "Do I have to give up sex forever?" This question is usually followed by a statement like: "If I have to give up sex permanently, then you can forget about me staying in recovery." And who would fault them for this as sex is, after all, a natural life affirming activity?

Fortunately, unlike sobriety for alcoholism and drug addiction, sexual sobriety is not defined by long-term abstinence. Instead, sexual addiction treatment addresses sobriety much as it is handled with eating disorders, another area in which long-term *abstinence* is simply not feasible. Essentially, instead of permanently abstaining from all sexual activity, recovering sex addicts learn to define and avoid being compulsive, problematic, objectified sexual behavior.

That said, sex addicts new to treatment and recovery are often asked to take a short timeout (usually thirty days or so) from all sexual behaviors, including masturbation during which they begin the process of healing. This brief period of total sexual abstinence is suggested because most have lost touch with reality when it comes to sexual behavior, and they therefore can find it incredibly difficult to distinguish between healthy and problematic attractions, flirtations, and, of course, sex. This period of temporary celibacy provides recovering sex addicts, working with a therapist or some other accountability partner, a chance to develop some clarity about which of their sexual behaviors are addictive and which are not. Sex addicts can also use this time to dismantle denial, to learn what their triggers are, and to develop healthy coping skills that they can turn to instead of acting out.

In much the same way that drug detox is a first step toward recovery from a substance addiction, this short period of complete sexual abstinence—a "detox" from addictive sex—is a first step toward recovery from sexual addiction. This time away from sex (along with flirting, porn, cruising, emotional affairs, etc.), interrupts long-established patterns of compulsive sexual behavior while clarity, ego strength, social skills, support networks, and new coping skills are developed. Again, celibacy is not a long-term goal. In truth, the heavy lifting of sex addiction recovery is not this period of self-restraint; but rather it's the slow (re)introduction of healthy sexuality and intimacy into the addict's life that takes the most work. In other words, the true goal of sexual recovery and sexual sobriety is not sexual celibacy; it's learning to meet one's emotional and physical needs without having to run to problematic sexual behavior as a quick fix for deeper issues.

Crafting a Personalized Definition
of Sexual Sobriety

WHEN GEORGE, A THIRTY-SEVEN-YEAR-OLD MUSICIAN, first sought help for sexual addiction, he didn't actually know what his goals were, or how he wanted his future life to look. He knew that his nightly ritual of hiring a prostitute after performing at a local club was problematic and that his secrecy around this behavior was driving a wedge between him and his wife. He admitted in treatment that he'd tried numerous times to stop seeing prostitutes, but he could never seem to manage for more than a week. George started his work by writing a non-graphic, but nonetheless fearless and complete sexual history, which he then read it to his accountability partner. This offered him objective insight into the reality of his problem. Thus, he was then more clear about what sexual behaviors needed to be entered onto his sobriety plan when he was asked to create one. And by then crafting (and being accountable to) this plan—writing down his problem activities, agreeing to abstain from those behaviors and finding someone to whom he would be accountable about his future sexual choices—that he was able to establish a foothold in recovery.

Many sex addicts new to the healing process openly wonder: "If sexual sobriety doesn't require priest-like celibacy what does it require?" Interestingly, there is no cut-and-dried answer to this question. Each sex addict arrives in recovery with a unique life history and set of problems, along with highly individualized goals for his or her future life. Thus, each sex addict, with the help of his or her therapist or some other accountability partner, must craft a personalized version of sexual sobriety.

To create a personalized version of sexual sobriety, sex addicts must first delineate the sexual behaviors that do and do not compromise and/or destroy their values (fidelity, not hurting others, etc.), life circumstances (keeping a job, not getting arrested, etc.), and relationships. Sex addicts then commit in a *written sexual sobriety contract**** to only engage in sexual behaviors that are nonproblematic (for them). As long as their sexual behavior does not violate these highly individualized boundaries, they are sexually sober. It is important that these plans be *put in writing*, and that they clearly define the addict's bottom-line problem behaviors. Murky plans lead to murky recovery as does lack of accountability.

Once again, the definition of sexual sobriety, because it takes into account each person's values, beliefs, goals, and life circumstances, is different for every sex addict. For instance, sexual sobriety for twenty-eight-year-old single gay men will probably look very different than sexual sobriety for a forty-eight-year-old married father of three. The goal is not conformity; the goal is a non-compulsive, non-secretive, non-shaming sexual life.

Crafting a Sexual Boundary Plan

Written sexual sobriety contracts often take the form of sexual boundary plans. These plans define and set limits on which sexual behaviors are and not acceptable for each individual sex addict. Typically, the process of crafting a sexual boundary plan begins with a statement of goals. Essentially, sex addicts list the primary reasons they want to change their sexual behavior. A few commonly stated goals include:

✓ I want to spend my free time having fun with friends and family.
✓ I don't want to cheat on or keep secrets from my spouse.

*** A sample can be found at the end of this chapter.

✓ I want to be present in the real world and find a loving relation-
  ship instead of living my life online.
✓ I don't want to abuse pornography ever again.
✓ I don't want to break the law anymore (prostitutes, viewing
  illicit images).
✓ I want to feel like a whole, integrated, healthy person, living my
  life with integrity, not lies and manipulations.
✓ I don't want to worry about STD's anymore.

Once an addict's goals for recovery are clearly stated, he or she
can move forward with the creation of a personalized sexual sobriety
plan, utilizing these preestablished goals as an overall guide. Sometimes sexual sobriety plans are simple, straightforward statements
like, "I will not engage in sexual infidelity no matter what," or, "I will
not view pornography of any kind." More often, though, sex addicts
require a more elaborate set of guidelines, typically a three-tiered
plan, constructed as follows:

THE INNER BOUNDARY: This is the addict's bottom-line definition of
sexual sobriety. Here a sex addict lists specific sexual behaviors (not
thoughts or fantasies) that are causing problems in his or her life and
that he or she therefore needs to stop. In other words, this boundary
lists the damaging and troublesome acts that have created negative life consequences and incomprehensible demoralization for the
addict. If the addict engages in inner boundary behaviors, he or she
has "slipped" and will need to reset his or her sobriety clock (while
also doing a thorough examination of what led to the slip). A few
common inner boundary behaviors are:

• Paying for sex
• Calling an ex for sex
• Going online for porn at work, home, or on my phone

- Masturbating to porn (video, online, paper or cable)
- Engaging in webcam sex (paid or free)
- Getting sensual massages or hiring prostitutes
- Hooking up for casual and/or anonymous sex
- Having affairs
- Exhibiting oneself (online and/or real world)
- Using apps to hook-up with strangers

THE MIDDLE BOUNDARY: This boundary lists warning signs and slippery situations that might lead a sex addict back to inner boundary activities (acting out). Here the addict lists the people, places, thoughts/fantasies, events, and experiences that might trigger his or her desire to act out sexually. In addition to obvious potential triggers (logging on to the Internet when alone, driving through a neighborhood where prostitutes hang out, downloading a hookup app, etc.), this list should include things that might indirectly trigger a desire to act out (working long hours, arguing with a spouse or boss, keeping secrets, worrying about finances, family holidays, etc.). A few common middle boundary items are:

- Skipping therapy and/or a support group meeting
- Lying (about anything), especially to a loved one
- Poor self-care (lack of sleep, eating poorly, forgoing exercise, etc.)
- Working more hours than usual or more intensely than usual
- Spending time with family of origin (holidays, reunions, etc.)
- Finding myself pushing those close to me away (irritability, fighting, creating unnecessary drama)
- Fighting and/or arguing with anyone, especially with loved ones
- Unstructured time alone
- Traveling alone (for any reason) without a plan to remain accountable

- Feeling lonely and unloved
- Feeling bored and restless

THE OUTER BOUNDARY: This boundary lists healthy behaviors and activities that can and hopefully will lead a sex addict toward his or her life goals, including things not at all limited to having a healthy, nondestructive sex life. These healthy pleasures are what the addict can turn to as a replacement for sexual acting out. Outer boundary activities may be immediate and concrete, such as "working on my house," or long-term and less tangible, such as "redefining my career goals." In all cases, the list should reflect a healthy combination of work community, recovery, and play. If going to a support group three or more times per week, exercising daily, and seeing a therapist one or more times per week are on the list, then spending time with friends, enjoying a hobby, and just plain relaxing should also be on the list. A few common (sample) outer boundary behaviors are:

- Spending more time with family, especially kids
- Reconnecting with old friends
- Rekindling an old hobby (or developing a new one)
- Getting in shape (exercise)—especially joining a team or group activity
- Getting regular sleep
- Working no more than eight hours per day
- Rejoining and becoming active in church/temple, etc.
- Going back to school
- Working on the house and yard—catching up on delayed plans
- Doing volunteer work

Once again, and I can't stress this enough, every sex addict is different. Each addict has a unique life history, singular goals, and specific problematic sexual behaviors. Therefore, every sexual boundary plan is different. Behaviors that are deeply troubling for one sex addict may be perfectly acceptable for another, and vice versa. As such, there is no set formula for defining and living sexual sobriety. The key is for each addict to be totally, completely, and brutally honest when formulating his or her boundary plan.

It is important to also state that sexual boundary plans are about much more than staying away from inner boundary items (problem behaviors). Yes, eliminating problem behaviors is a primary and ongoing goal of recovery, but as the plan itself suggests, there is much more involved with the healing process than simply eliminating problem behaviors. That part should be considered a given. Over the long term, recovering from sexual addiction is much more about truly learning how to enjoy your life, while healthfully coping with its daily ups and downs. After all, the outer boundary (above) defines the way in which the addict wants to live his or her life. *Put simply, no addict ever fully recovers simply by not doing certain things.* The flip side is equally important. *The more positive things a person does to feel good about his or herself and life, the better their life will be.*

About Masturbation

When crafting a sexual boundary plan, one potentially tricky gray area is masturbation. For many sex addicts, masturbation is an integral part of the addictive cycle, directly feeding the fantasies that produce the "high" of sexual addiction. In such cases, masturbation is either a slippery, but still-sober, middle-boundary behavior, or a bottom-line, inner-boundary behavior. For other sex addicts, non-compulsive masturbation may actually aid recovery, encouraging appropriate intimacy, and contributing to an overall sense of sexual health and well-being. For instance, masturbating while being held by one's partner can be, for some couples, an incredibly intimate act. In such cases, occasional masturbation may (or may not) be okay. At the other end of the spectrum, returning to masturbation via endless objectified images (à la Internet porn and/or sexting) will most likely remain off the table for some time, if not permanently.

Given the confusion about masturbation and where to place it within one's plan, recovering sex addicts should always discuss the issue with their therapist or some other accountability partner, preferably erring on the side of caution. In any case a return to masturbation in any case is best discussed prior to any action taken.

When first crafted, sexual boundary plans typically look airtight. However, they usually are not. And even when they are, many sex addicts find ways to manipulate and work around their plans. Knowing this, it is wise to keep the following tips in mind when constructing and implementing a sexual sobriety plan.

✓ **Be clear and specific.** Boundary plans are intended to define sexual sobriety and to provide a plan for a healthier, happier life. They are *written and signed as contracts* as a way to hold sex addicts accountable to their commitments, particularly in the face of challenging circumstances. When sex addicts lack clearly written boundaries, they are vulnerable to deciding in the moment that certain activities are okay for now even though they've been wildly problematic in the past. Remember, impulsive sexual decisions made without clear guidelines are what dragged the addict down in the first place, so it's best to not leave any wiggle room in sobriety, especially in the first year.

✓ **Be flexible (over time).** Boundary plans are not set in stone. In fact, recovering sex addicts often spend a month or two (or a year or two) with a particular set of boundaries and then realize that their plan needs adjustment. (Recent developments in digital technology have forced many long-sober sex addicts to revise their boundary plans.) That said, changing a boundary plan is never something an addict should do on his or her own. Making changes should always involve input from the addict's therapist, twelve-step sponsor, and/or accountability partner. Changes to boundary plans are not made just because some "special situation" presents itself and the addict decides, in the moment, to make a change. Such behavior is not called "changing the plan," it's called "acting out."

✓ **Be honest.** Creating effective boundary plans requires complete and brutal honesty on the part of not just the addict, but his or her advisors. Let's face it, if an addict is looking to justify the continuation of a particular behavior, even though he or she knows that it no longer serves a healthy purpose, that person can nearly always find someone to sign off on it (or at least to agree that it's not a big deal). It is important to remember here that the purpose of creating a sexual boundary plan is not to justify and rationalize problematic behaviors (or even watered-down versions of those activities), the purpose is to end sexual acting out and the incomprehensible demoralization it brings.

✓ **Consider others.** Sex addicts who develop their boundary plans while single often find that they need to revise their plans if/when they enter into a serious relationship. Sex addicts already in long-term relationships need to consider how their new boundaries will affect their partner. Explaining to that person the reasons for these seemingly sudden changes in intimate relating will usually soften the impact.

Do Sex Addicts Experience Withdrawal?

It is common knowledge that alcoholics and drug addicts, when they suddenly go "cold turkey," often experience withdrawal, things like: delirium tremens (the DTs), chills, fevers, insomnia, night sweats, headaches, nausea, diarrhea, tachycardia (elevated heart rate), hypertension, depression, agitation, anxiety, hallucinations, irritability, and the like. Withdrawal from some substances is worse than withdrawal from others. Opiate addiction (including addiction to heroin) and alcoholism tend to produce the worst physical symptoms. Sometimes these symptoms can actually be life-threatening if not medically managed.[1]

Typically, substance addicts dealing with severe physical withdrawal symptoms are "titrated" off their drug of choice, meaning they are given a medication that "manages" their withdrawal by temporarily replacing their addictive drug of choice, and then they are slowly but steadily weaned off of that medication. Usually this process takes anywhere from a few days to a few weeks.

But what about sexual addiction. Do sex addicts get the DTs and hallucinate the same as alcoholics and heroin addicts? Typically they do not. This does not, however, mean that a sudden stoppage of addictive sexual fantasy and activity does not produce withdrawal. In fact, it nearly always does to some degree. Most often withdrawal from sexual addiction manifests as one or more of the following:

✓ **Irritability, anxiety, agitation, depression, etc.:** Most sex addicts experience extreme emotional discomfort in early sobriety. And why not? After all, addictive sexuality has been their primary way of coping with any and all discomfort—including feelings as seemingly benign as boredom—for years on end. When the addiction is taken away, they no longer have this easy means of numbing out and escaping. And without that, they must face their emotions head-on. For people who've been trying to "not feel" for years or even decades, this can be an incredibly uncomfortable experience both for them and those around them.

✓ **A desire to explore other potential addictions:** Many sex addicts new to recovery find themselves replacing (or longing to replace) their sexual addiction with some other compulsive (and highly distracting) activity. Sometimes this manifests as a cross-addiction. For instance, a sex addict who suddenly stops acting out experiences a corresponding flood of uncomfortable emotions (as discussed above), and without compulsive sexuality to stem the tide, he or she may turn to drinking, drugging, smoking, eating, gambling, spending, or any other pleasurable substance or behavior. Knowing this, it is incredibly important that recovering sex addicts keep a watchful eye on other pleasure inducing behaviors, especially in the first few months of the recovery process.

✓ **Loneliness and longing for connection:** For most sex addicts, sexual acting out masks not only day-to-day stress and emotional discomfort, but underlying issues related to a longing for intimacy. Without the constant distraction of sexual fantasy and activity, this longer-term condition can rise to the surface and cause intense feelings of loneliness, fear, isolation, and unhappiness. These feelings are perfectly normal and to be expected. After all, sex addicts are grieving the loss of their primary long-term relationship (their addiction), and they naturally feel a need to replace it.

In the Beginning—It Takes Work

In early sexual sobriety, even the smallest annoyance can feel like a major issue. Without their go-to coping mechanism, recovering sex addicts have a tendency to overreact and blow up. They get angry with themselves and others, they cry, get defensive, they're afraid, they're lonely, etc. As such, sex addicts in early recovery are not always fun to be around. This is their emotional withdrawal.

Conversely, some sex addicts experience the opposite of withdrawal in early recovery. This is known as the *honeymoon* or the *pink cloud*. These lucky individuals find that when they embark on the path of healing, they suddenly lose all desire to act out sexually. They are fascinated by the insight they are developing, and thrilled to have finally found a solution to their deepest problem and someone to help.

This *temporary* phase of early recovery is great while it lasts. However, sex addicts who are riding the pink cloud should be aware that their desire to sexually act out will return, and it may be stronger than ever when it does. If this eventuality is not anticipated and prepared for, it is easy to either relapse or to think that something has gone wrong in the healing process. In reality, there is no need for relapse, and nothing is amiss with recovery. Instead, this is a normal part of the process and the addict is simply experiencing a delayed form of withdrawal.

Any sex addict who recognizes that he or she is experiencing symptoms of withdrawal should talk about those feelings with a supportive person who is knowledgeable about the sex addiction cycle. Most often this person will be a therapist, a twelve-step sponsor, or a friend in recovery. It is often useful to be evaluated for depression or anxiety by a medical professional. Close friends not in recovery and family members can also be helpful. If symptoms of withdrawal are extreme (especially depression, dissociation, and/or anxiety), a licensed mental health professional should be consulted as soon as possible. Severe unchecked withdrawal symptoms can lead not only to sex addiction relapse but to other forms of serious self-harm.

Your Turn: Creating a Sexual Sobriety Plan

Goals: Each boundary plan starts with a listing of goals (i.e., reasons for change). Please write down five or more goals for your sexual recovery.

Example: I don't want to cheat on my spouse ever again.

1) _____

2) _____

3) _____

4) _____

5) _____

Inner Boundary: The inner boundary lists the bottom-line sexual behaviors you need to stop. These are the activities (not thoughts) that are causing problems in your life. Please list here all of the behaviors that drove you into recovery—the activities that you need to stop and stop now.

Example: Looking at and masturbating to pornography (of any kind).

1) _____

2) _____

3) _____

4) _____

5) _____

6) _____

7) _____

8) _____

9) _____

10) _____

Middle Boundary: The middle boundary lists warning signs and slippery situations that might lead you back to inner-boundary activities. Please list here the people, places, thoughts/fantasies, events, and experiences that might either directly or indirectly trigger your desire to act out sexually.

Example: Keeping secrets from anyone, especially my spouse.

1) _____

2) _____

3) _____

4) _____

5) _____

6) _____

7) _____

8) _____

9) _____

10) _____

Outer Boundary: The outer boundary lists healthy behaviors and activities that can and hopefully will lead you toward your short- and long-term life goals, including but not even remotely limited to having a healthy, nondestructive sex life. Please list here the healthy behaviors you can turn to as a replacement for your sexual acting out.

Example: I want to spend more time with my friends and family, especially my children.

1) _____

2) _____

3) _____

4) _____

5) _____

6) _____

7) _____

8) _____

9) _____

10) _____

11

Finding Therapeutic Help and Healing

MELISSA, A FIFTY-YEAR-OLD mother of three, really wants her third marriage to be a lasting one. She has worked as a flight attendant for nearly thirty years. From the very beginning of that job, men would occasionally proposition her on flights, and once in a while she would take them up on their offers, even though she was married. Her first husband never found out about this; they got divorced because of his cheating, not hers. Nor did her second husband find out; they got divorced because he was physically abusive when he drank (and he drank every day). Over the past few years, ever since Melissa first heard about Ashley Madison and various other hookup apps, the frequency of her illicit liaisons has increased, even though she's now married to husband number three (who neither cheats nor drinks). She now finds herself flirting and cheating almost daily when on the road, despite the fact that she really loves her new husband and wants them to stay together for the long haul. So far, because of her travel schedule, she's been able to hide her ever-increasing sexual infidelities, but she feels as if her life is spinning out of control, and that she's pulling away from her husband and her kids. She worries that another divorce is inevitable, and that this time it will be her fault rather than her husband's. Depressed and filled with anxiety, she is nevertheless resistant to therapy because she thinks it won't help. She thinks this because her vision of therapy consists of sitting in a room with a pipe-smoking man who says things like, "Tell me about your relationship with your mother," and, "*Hmmm*, I see," and, "How do you feel about that?" Melissa doesn't want help with her child-hood issues, whatever they may be; she wants active, directed help with her in-the-moment sexual behavior and her marriage.

Melissa is far from the only sex addict to resist seeking treatment for sexual addiction because she doesn't understand the process and therefore thinks it won't help. In reality, sex addiction treatment is straightforward, beginning with with a very "here and now" focus on the identification and containment of present-day problematic sexual and romantic behaviors, leaving the past in the past until the client is ready (and wants) to deal with it. Furthermore, if the addict is motivated, engaged, and willing to take direction, the likelihood of long-term success is quite good. In an effort to alleviate misperceptions about the therapeutic treatment of sex addicts, this chapter presents a simple, point-by-point explanation of the process.

Generally speaking, sexual addiction treatment utilizes the same basic motivational strategies and task-oriented techniques that work with drug and alcohol addiction. For the most part, early treatment focuses on a very thorough life/relationship/sexual history, breaking though denial, managing the crisis or crises that drove the addict into recovery, and relapse prevention. Techniques utilized typically include individual and group therapy—most often a highly directive, behaviorally focused form of psychotherapy like cognitive behavioral therapy (CBT), coupled with psycho-education, social learning, twelve-step and/or other addiction-focused social support. Once sobriety and some level of life stability is achieved, there is potential, depending on the client, to add in various alternative therapeutic modalities like art and movement therapies, psychodrama, equine therapy, exercise, meditation, eye movement desensitization and reprocessing (EMDR), etc. Following professional evaluation, some clients may also begin a trial run of an antidepressant or anti-anxiety medication, as these medications *sometimes* help to reduce not only depression and anxiety, as well as emotional reactivity but also cravings (to act out sexually).

If some of this stuff sounds confusing, don't worry, I'll clarify as this chapter progresses.

Inpatient and/or Intensive Outpatient Treatment

Despite their initial resistance, many (perhaps most) recovering sex addicts do seek some form of professional assistance and good for them. For many of these men and women, inpatient rehab and/or intensive outpatient treatment serves as the initial step on the pathway to healing. The length of these programs varies depending on the treatment facility, typically running anywhere from two weeks to two months. To achieve long-term success, these intensive programs should be followed up with outpatient therapy paired with twelve-step, faith-based, and/or other forms of support groups.

(This process is very much in line with treatment for other forms of addiction.)

One common misconception about inpatient and intensive out-patient treatment for sexual addiction is that after completing the recommended program, sex addicts will never again struggle with problematic sexual behaviors. This is not in fact the case. In reality, there is no cure for sexual addiction (or any other addiction), and sex addicts will battle the issue at various levels of struggle on an ongoing, lifelong basis. The desire to act out sexually, when experiencing emotional stress and the unexpected turns life takes, does not go away. It lessens, certainly, and recovering sex addicts learn to respond in healthy ways when triggered, but the desire to engage in the addiction does not disappear entirely, no matter how good the treatment center or how motivated the addict especially when stress shows up. So rather than trying to cure sex addicts, treatment programs focus on the following:

- ✓ Helping sex addicts determine which of their sexual behaviors are problematic and which are not
- ✓ Creating awareness of and helping addicts distance themselves from the people, places, and things that trigger their problematic sexual behavior patterns
- ✓ Reducing sex addicts' denial by helping them gain insight into the full extent of their past dependency on sexual fantasy and behavior as a means of distraction and emotional self-stabilization
- ✓ Educating sex addicts about the full extent of their consequences, looking at harm not only to themselves, but to their family, friends, employers, and others
- ✓ Identifying sex addicts' triggers and developing relapse prevention tools that they can utilize when those triggers arise

- ✓ Coaching and supporting sex addicts while they build the ego strength, social skills, and support network necessary for lasting sexual sobriety
- ✓ Breaking through sex addicts' resistance to participation in life-long, ongoing recovery and healing from sexual addiction
- ✓ Working to address underlying early trauma negelect, and abuse
- ✓ Encouraging healthy long-term lifestyle changes and self care, stress reduction, increased healthy recreation, and new ways to simply have "fun" without intensity.

As stated above, residential and/or intensive outpatient treatment is often the first step on the road to long-term sobriety and a healthier, happier life. However, these intensive programs *do not cure addiction*. Instead, they help addicts to break their long-established behavior patterns and to begin the process of building needed awareness and coping skills. In short, intensive treatment programs, both inpatient and outpatient, are meant to prepare addicts for the lifelong work to come. (therapy, self care, community support, etc.)

The Therapeutic Process

It is not unusual for sex addicts starting treatment to expect that much of their work in therapy, whatever the setting, will focus on the identification and resolution of childhood issues via traditional talk therapy. (This is why Melissa, in an earlier example, was so resistant to treatment.) And even though addressing early-life trauma is often an aspect of sexual addiction treatment, it's just one among many, and it's usually not an initial priority. Other concerns, mostly involving client safety and present-day behaviors, are always paramount early in the process.

So what does happen in psychotherapeutic treatment for sexual addiction?

Individual Therapy

The progression of addiction treatment is actually quite logical. The first step is a thorough bio-psycho-sexual-social assessment. This careful evaluation explores and evaluates nearly every aspect of the addict's life, including his or her sex and relationship history. Individuals are assessed not just for sexual addiction but for other psychological issues (including other addictions), along with relationship, family, legal, work, social, recreational, and financial concerns that may need to be dealt with.

Typically, as stated earlier, the preferred methodology in sexual addiction treatment is cognitive behavioral therapy (CBT). CBT differs from traditional talk therapy, in that it is moe proactive and directive. This highly focused accountability-based approach recognizes that sexual addiction, like all other addictions, is a behavioral problem, and it therefore responds best to behavioral forms of treatment.

With CBT, the work of therapy is reality based, focusing on the sex addict's behaviors and well-being in the here and now, instead of looking at and seeking to resolve past traumas. As such, the process is task-oriented, with assignments (reading, writing, attending support groups, etc.) to be completed between sessions and discussed during sessions.

Group Therapy

Typically, healing from sexual addiction presents challenges that can't be dealt with solely in individual, one-on-one therapy. In fact, sex addicts nearly always require external reinforcement and support if they want to permanently change their deeply rooted patterns of behavior. Sex addiction-focused group therapy can be extremely helpful in this regard. Generally, a treatment specialist works with between six and ten same-gender sex addicts. (Co-ed sex addiction therapy groups are, for obvious reasons, a bad idea.) Generally these groups run ninety minutes to two hours per session. Sexual orientation is not considered part of this equation, meaning that men work in groups with men, regardless of orientation, and the same goes for women. These types of groups help promote healthy, intimate (but nonsexual) same-sex bonds and relationships, and thus it is a primary treatment method.

Group therapy helps sex addicts learn that their problems are not unique (thus they feel less alone), which goes a long way toward reducing the shame associated with their behaviors. It is also the ideal place to confront the denial that is so integral to sexual addiction. Such confrontations are powerful, not only for the addict being confronted, but for the addicts doing the confronting. In this fashion, everyone present learns how justification, minimization, and rationalization sustain sexual addiction. Addicts are also able to learn which interventions and coping mechanisms work best based on other members' experiences. Most important, sex addicts learn that helpful support and direction are available from many caring people, not just a primary therapist or a lone accountability partner.

Twelve-Step Sexual Recovery Groups

In addition to individual and group therapy, sex addicts who are willing to push beyond their fear of "being seen" in a more public (though anonymous) setting will nearly always benefit from twelve-step sexual recovery meetings. Sexaholics Anonymous (SA), Sex Addicts Anonymous (SAA), Sexual Compulsives Anonymous (SCA), Sex and Love Addicts Anonymous (SLAA), and Sexual Recovery Anonymous (SRA) are nationwide programs in which sex addicts can find non-shaming, nonreligious peer support and guidance. Generally speaking, SCA is the most "gay friendly" program, and SLAA is the most "female friendly" program. Some meetings are open to anyone who wishes to attend, while others are open only to those who identify as sexually addicted. A few meetings are gender- or sexual-orientation specific. It is best to check ahead by looking meetings up online or calling the group's local hotline number. (For more information about twelve-step groups and how they work, see the Resources chapter.)

Sometimes recovering sex addicts resist attending and/or participating in twelve-step recovery groups. Usually they're worried about a loss of privacy. Frankly, it's more than slightly ironic that people who act out sexually—often in very public ways (putting nude pics on dating sites and hookup apps, hiring prostitutes, having affairs, etc.)—are suddenly worried about what other people will think if they are "caught," standing outside a church, school or recreation hall. Plus, the odds of being talked about after attending a twelve-step meeting are actually rather slim. Honestly, what sex addict wants to say to others, "I was at this sex addiction meeting the other evening talking about my porn problem and guess who I saw there?"

Certainly twelve-step sexual recovery groups are not as confidential as a therapist's office, but the word "anonymous" is part of the title, and anonymity is heavily talked about and encouraged in most meetings. And again, if anyone sees you at one of these groups, it's because that person is there for the same basic reasons as you, and he or she probably doesn't want to be gossiped about any more than you do.

Finding the Right Therapist

SANDRO, A THIRTY-FIVE-YEAR-OLD WRITER, saw three different therapists before he found someone who actually helped him with his problematic patterns of compulsive sexual activity. His first therapist, (even though Sandro stated very clearly that his loss of control over hookup apps had cost him several good relationships) and more recently, his job, just saw him as a relatively young man with a healthy sexual appetite. Instead of looking at Sandro as a possible sex addict, this therapist encouraged him to accept his "need for sexual fulfillment." Sandro worked hard at this, but his issues worsened and he fell into a deep depression. He eventually recognized that this therapist wasn't helping him, so he sought help elsewhere, this time with a clinician specializing in men with depression. This therapist never even asked about Sandro's sex life. Instead, he focused entirely on techniques for dealing with depression, and on uncovering and resolving Sandro's childhood trauma issues. Unfortunately, discussing childhood traumas left Sandro more emotionally raw than ever, thus his sexual acting out escalated even further. Eventually, he read an online article discussing sexual addiction, written by a certified sex addiction treatment specialist. He immediately began his search for a similarly credentialed therapist in his town, finding several. Once he was being treated for his primary disorder, sexual addiction, he felt immediately better about himself, as he felt both understood and was given tools to help with behavior change. Thus, his depression lifted and his need to act out diminished significantly.

Unfortunately for sex addicts, the process of locating a qualified treatment specialist is not always easy. For starters, a basic understanding of sexual addiction is not a standard part of the training for most psychotherapists. As such, sex addicts sometimes encounter therapists who are unfamiliar with sexual addiction but knowledgeable about various related and co-occurring issues, most notably: trauma, depression, family systems, and relationship problems. These clinicians often correctly diagnose and then treat these secondary issues while never quite touching on the addict's primary concern, which is their problem sexual behavior, because the professional has not been trained to assess or treat this. So they mistakenly end up misidentifying the issue as a mood or relationship problem, not knowing about or not addressing the client's active sexual behavior patterns. These

may be highly skilled, caring professionals, who simply don't understand what they are treating. Add to this the fact that clients, often
feeling shameful about their behavior, will minimize, and dismiss
the extent of their sexual acting out—especially with a therapist who
seems disinclined or even uncomfortable bringing it up.

Put simply, mood disorders (depression, anxiety, and the like) are
far more common than sexual addiction, and therapists are generally well-trained when it comes to diagnosing and treating them.
Thus, these *common side effects* of sexual addiction get misidentified
as the primary issue. And even when a therapist knows about the
addict's out-of-control sexual activity, the addict can still rather easily
be misdiagnosed, with bipolar disorder, obsessive-compulsive disorder
(OCD), a dissociative disorder, or even attention-deficit/hyperactiv-
ity disorder (ADHD)—any and all of which can manifest with an
element of sexual compulsivity.[1] Nevertheless, these disorders are not
usually an underlying condition for many sex addicts. In fact, issues
such as depression and anxiety that manifest in conjunction with
sexual addiction often alleviated or at least minimized once the addict
achieves a modicum of sexual sobriety, as we saw in the example with
Sandro above.

About Sex Therapists

While one might think that someone certified as a "sex therapist"
surely would understand the issue of sexual addiction, this is often not
the case. Sex therapists are generally trained to be fully "sex positive,"
meaning their goal is to help people feel better about their sexual
interests or patterns, rather than trying to eliminate those interests
and patterns. And while this type of validating, supportive, nonjudgmental treatment can be a highly effective approach when managing
other sexual issues, such as feeling uncomfortable about sex in general, same-sex attractions, gender identity issues, or a fetish of some

sort, this type of well-intentioned advice is *counterproductive for sex addicts*, as we saw with Sandro and his first therapist. These clinicians tend to offer advice like, "What if we helped you to just loosen up and to become more comfortable with your sexuality." This, of course, is the exact opposite of what a sex addict needs to hear. Imagine, if you will, a therapist telling an alcoholic with two arrests for drunk driving while intoxicated to loosen up a bit and drink without shame! Well, this is what sex therapists often unknowingly do with sex addicts.

At the other end of the spectrum there are misguided mental health professionals who will label a person as sexually addicted as a way to marginalize and pathologize sexual activity that does not mesh with their personal or religious belief system. In essence, these therapists are trying to be the "sex police," imposing broad-brush moral, cultural, and/or religious values on human sexuality, thereby creating a narrow version of sexual health. Many such therapists routinely misapply the sex addiction diagnosis, using it to "treat" homosexuality, bisexuality, recreational porn use, casual sex, non-monogamy, fetishes, kink, and a wide variety of other sexual behaviors that fall well within the boundaries of normal and healthy adult sexuality (even if the client is uncomfortable with those desires and/or behaviors).

Needless to say, finding the right therapist is imperative, because the wrong one can inadvertently do much more harm than good. As such, when choosing a therapist, sex addicts should look not so much at the clinician's academic degrees, but at whether that person is certified in and/or has extensive experience with the treatment of *sexual* addiction. A "CSAT" designation (for "certified sex addiction therapist") after the clinician's name is one primary indicator of these qualifications. If a sex addict is already attending twelve-step support group meetings, he or she might ask around for referrals. If already in therapy, targeted SA treatment can be adjunctive. Otherwise, the addict may consider the International Institute for Trauma and

Addiction Professionals website, (*iitap.com*), or SASH, the Society for the Advancement of Sexual Health (*sash.org*), for referrals. IITAP is the organization that offers CSAT training and certification; the website lists certified therapists by city and state. Other places to seek help are listed in the Resources chapter.

Evaluating a Potential Therapist

Before entering any therapeutic relationship, it is wise to make sure that a particular clinician is the right fit. You should feel comfortable (not shamed or devalued) and understood (supported and guided) by this person, and you should feel as if he or she has the requisite knowledge and experience to help you. If you are dealing with sexual addiction, you also need a therapist who will professionally confront you about your behaviors and your distorted thinking (your denial), even when holding you accountable feels uncomfortable. Asking certain questions either prior to or during the initial session can be quite helpful in terms of choosing the right therapist. A few sample questions for a potential sex addiction therapist include:

- ✓ Are you trained in the diagnosis and treatment of sexual addiction? If so, what training have you received?
- ✓ Do you have experience working with sexually addicted clients? If so, to what extent?
- ✓ Have you helped clients with other addictions such as alcoholism, drug addiction, and the like?
- ✓ Do you recommend that your sexually addicted clients attend twelve-step recovery meetings and/or a support group? (Most good sex addiction therapists will say they not only recommend this, they insist on it.)
- ✓ Do you offer sex-addiction focused group therapy and/or recommend it to your clients? (Again, most good sex addiction

therapists will say they not only recommend this, they insist on it and can help guide clients to it.)

✓ How would you help me if I relapsed? (Good sex addiction therapists take a non-shaming approach that looks at the underlying causes of the relapse and how the addict might avoid similar relapses in the future.)

✓ If applicable: are you comfortable working with gay and lesbian clients?

✓ If applicable: how will you address or handle my religious beliefs?

✓ If applicable: what kind of direction and/or support can you offer my spouse? (Typically, good sex addiction therapists will suggest that your spouse see a different therapist, so long as that other therapist is knowledgeable about sexual addiction and experienced in working with spouses of sex addicts.) Note that spousal involvement is essential to a couple's healing.

As much as you may want to find someone who can help you *right now*—especially if you are in the midst of an addiction-related crisis—it is a good idea to interview more than one potential clinician before deciding whom to see. And there is nothing wrong with doing this. In fact, good therapists understand the need for a mutual fit, and they will not be offended if you choose someone else. The best clinicians sometimes encourage potential clients to sit with several people before making a decision on who suits them and their situation the best.

Couples Treatment

Sex addicts who are in a long-term relationship when they enter recovery and begin the process of healing may want to consider, in addition to individual and group therapy, couples counseling. Usually it is best if the therapist is familiar with sexual addiction and the process of healing. Otherwise, he or she may be highly reactive to the sex addict's disclosures (even taking sides as a result), and this helps nobody. And sometimes these clinicians simply don't understand that partners of sex addicts, despite their anger and hurt, are often not anywhere near ready to end the relationship.

As such, it is critical to find a couples counselor who understands the basics of sexual addiction and is willing to work toward the couple's individual and relationship goals, whatever those goals might be. In other words, the clinician should be able to objectively and impartially hear both the addict's and the betrayed partner's stories, responding to them without judgment or a hidden agenda.

With couples counseling, it is always best to work with a therapist who has a "no secrets" policy, meaning he or she will work to facilitate the process of disclosure rather than working to protect one or both parties from full knowledge about the addiction. Though it may be effective to hold on to some information until it is ready to be healthfully disclosed, a good therapist will promise not to keep any secrets in the long run. More about couples healing to come.

To close, a reminder here, there is no cure for addiction. Similarly, there is no cure for complex trauma, depression, or anxiety. Treatment for these issues does not make them go away, never to return. Instead, treatment provides people with knowledge, skills, and tools that can reduce the power and impact of addiction and related issue(s), allowing the individual to live a healthier, happier, more connected, and more emotionally fulfilling life. The treatment goal for addiction of all kinds is more like cancer treatment, where the goal is healthy, long-term remission from a chronic symptom or problem. Those who expect the endpoint of addiction treatment to be a cure (like setting a broken bone that then mends permanently), are holding out unduly high expectations of the process.

12

Loving
a Sex Addict

MARINA, A TWENTY-NINE-YEAR-OLD fitness instruc-
tor, has been married to Justin, a professional martial
arts trainer, for nearly five years. When they got married,
they agreed to sexual fidelity. "We didn't want to be like
some of the other couples we knew who were sleeping
around all over the place," Marina says. "We promised
each other to be honest and to have integrity around our
sex life." And Marina has stood by that agreement. Justin,
however, seems to view monogamy as something to be
worked around rather than respected. Almost since the
day they were married he's been extensively looking at
pornography without his wife's knowledge and having
webcam sexual encounters. And lately he is devoting
more time and energy to those behaviors than to his
intimate life with Marina. "I can't take it anymore," she says,
"because he just keeps getting worse. In the beginning
I felt a little jilted, but back then I bought his lies about
how "a little bit of pornography doesn't count because it's

not real women," and then later I bought his lies about how webcam sex doesn't count as cheating because the woman lives a thousand miles away. Thus they will never meet up in real time. But now, I get it, *he's cheating*. I mean, if it walks like a duck and quacks like a duck, it's a duck. So he's cheating on me." At this point, Marina is extremely frustrated and unclear how to proceed with her marriage because when she broaches the topic with Justin, he either gets angry and defensive, or he belittles her and threatens to leave.

Is Your Partner a Sex Addict?

Most people think that if they were partnered with a sex addict, they would automatically know it. They incorrectly believe that it would be almost impossible to miss the signs of sexual addiction. But in truth, *the closer a person is to the problem, the harder it is to spot the problem.* Essentially, spouses don't want to believe that their closest ally could profoundly betray and harm them, and who would? So they tend to look the other way and make excuses for problem behaviors only to themselves "end up" in denial about what is happening. Knowing this, it actually makes sense that the betrayed spouse is usually the last to know about the infidelity. Besides, most people think that sex addicts are creepy men who hang out in adult bookstores, porno theaters, and in red-light districts—"obvious" perverts, so to speak, not like "my husband."

In reality, only a very small percentage of sex addicts fit this "low bottom," street-person stereotype. The rest are people that most of us deal with in our day-to-day lives, often regularly, without awareness of their addiction. This is because the vast majority of sex addicts work very hard to hide their problem (primarily because they don't want anything or anyone to interfere with their addictive sexual fantasies and behaviors, and because of the profound shame they often carry about them). As such, most sex addicts are at least relatively functional, maintaining jobs and even marriages while keeping their problem hidden.

Of course, the people around sex addicts are usually fairly helpful in this regard. This is because most of us, regardless of whether we are addicted, naturally want to keep our problems quiet and out of sight. In return, we are inclined to "not notice" the mildly, unusual, and/or occasionally erratic behaviors of other people—especially those we love. And when we do notice, instead of having the bad taste to mention these issues, we create in our own minds excuses for what the other person is doing. This is especially true in family settings, where healthy spouses *need to believe* their significant other is trustworthy, dependable and doing right by them as they should believe. In other words, loving family, spouses, even friends, are often unconsciously adept at "looking the other way." Because of this, many addicts are able to act out for years while loving spouses slog through a denial-driven fog, as those around them either don't recognize the problem, choose to ignore it or can't imagine it could be true.

Spotting Addiction—of Any Type

If you are worried that your spouse or partner may be an addict (of any type), there are several common issues to look for. Any and all of these signs can be indicative of addiction, though none is definitive in terms of saying, "Yes, my spouse is an addict." If, however, you spot several of these behaviors in a loved one, it may be time to take action.

✓ **Deceitfulness:** Active addicts are excellent liars. They fib and make excuses with cold, calculated precision, especially when it comes to protecting their addictive behaviors. When confronted about their lies, they deny, justify, minimize, and externalize by placing the blame on others (a spouse, a boss, a parent, a friend, the government, etc.)

✓ **Manipulation/Gaslighting:** Addicts hide their addiction by convincing you to believe their story—however unlikely it may be—rather than trusting your own feelings and intuition. They are incredibly persistent with this; they will keep at it until you wear down and give in. Often, they will try to make you feel as if *you* are the one with a problem (lack of trust, imagining things, etc.).

✓ **Mood Swings:** Some addicts can seem hyperactive and extremely happy, followed by periods of depression, irritability, and lethargy. Other addicts can seem pleasant and mellow, followed by periods of anxiety, paranoia, and anger. All this without an obvious external reason. Usually, if questioned, they blame these mood swings on the actions of others or on events beyond their control.

✓ **Physical Isolation and Withdrawal:** The easiest way to keep an addiction secret is to hide from anyone who might recognize the problem. Sometimes addicts just disappear completely. Later, of course, they tell their loved ones (and others) semi-plausible lies and stories to explain their absence.

✓ **Emotional Isolation and Withdrawal:** Because they tend to withdraw physically, and because they tend to be so unpredictably moody, addicts nearly always struggle with interpersonal relationships. As a result, they are notoriously non-intimate, rarely sharing their feelings or their problems.

✓ **Trouble at Work or in School:** Over time, addicts lose focus on just about everything that doesn't involve their addiction. As such, work and school tend to suffer. However, many addicts are able to "keep up appearances" in these arenas for long periods, sometimes for years on end, even though they're operating at much less than full capacity. Typically, the decline here is slow and difficult to notice, but it is almost always present.

✓ **Financial Issues:** Active addictions cost money. Even addicts with jobs that pay extremely well tend to live on the edge financially. Some become habitually late paying their bills, while others will ignore their financial obligations altogether or use funds saved for retirement, etc., toward sexual acting out. They may tell loved ones blatant lies about family finances to conceal their actual spending habits.

✓ **Declining Physical and/or Emotional Health:** Active addicts often experience either an increase or a decrease in appetite and/or sleep. Sometimes they binge and purge with one, the other, or both. Usually, because of this, their appearance declines directly related to (less self-care, less exercise, poor eating, sleep problems, etc.) The signs will look different depending on the addict, with sexual disorders manifesting much differently than, say, alcoholism or an eating disorder. As with work and school issues, changes to health and appearance are usually gradual and therefore difficult to notice, but they are almost always there.

Spotting Sexual Addiction

In addition to signs and symptoms common to all addictions, described above, sex addicts tend to show a few behavior-specific traits. Again, none of these is definitive in terms of saying, "Yes, my spouse is a sex addict," but if you spot more than one, you may want to take action or at least pay a lot more attention to what you are seeing and hearing.

✓ **Sexual and/or Romantic Secrets:** Sex addicts lie and keep secrets about their sexual and romantic activity. If caught in a lie, they typically attempt to cover it with still more lies. They seem to not care that this upsets their loved ones. Spouses and partners often feel unimportant and disrespected because the addict's sexual philandering seems more important to the addict than the sanctity of their primary relationship.

✓ **Failure to Keep Promises Regarding Sexual Activity:** Sex addicts often promise their loved ones that they will change their sexual and romantic behaviors. Sometimes they even follow through for a few days or weeks, but eventually they're right back at it.

✓ **Sexual and/or Romantic Detachment (emotional withdrawal):** Sex addicts are consistently more sexually and emotionally involved with porn, virtual sex, online chat, smartphone apps, and sexual and romantic intrigue (either online or in person) than with the loving spouse they have at home. Thus they tend to emotionally distance themselves from those closest to them.

✓ **Unwillingness to Discuss Sexual Behavioral Issues:** Sex addicts typically don't want to talk about their behavior and/or its consequences, or to consider changing their behavior. Their consistent reaction to concern about their sexual and romantic dalliances may be anger, denial, defensiveness, and/or blaming. They seem to not care how upsetting this is to their loved ones.

Recognizing Infidelity in the Digital Age

A few years ago, Dr. Jennifer Schneider, Dr. Charles Samenow, and I conducted a survey of men and women whose spouses or long-term partners were engaging in significant amounts of sexual activity, either online or real world, outside of their supposedly monogamous primary relationship. Probably the most important finding of our study was that *when it comes to the negative emotional effects of sex outside a supposedly monogamous relationship for the spouse, tech-based and in-the-flesh sexuality are no different.*[1] The lying, the emotional distancing, and the pain of learning about the betrayal all feel exactly the same to the betrayed partner, whether carried out in the virtual or real worlds.

The results of our study confirmed in many ways what I've said and written about infidelity for many years—that it's not any specific sexual act that does the most damage to the betrayed partner and the relationship; it's the constant lying, the emotional distancing, and the rending apart of relationship trust. In other words, emotional betrayal is nearly always more painful and longer-lasting than any actual physical betrayal. This long-held belief, coupled with the findings in our study, has led me to formulate the following modern-day definition of sexual infidelity:

> *Sexual infidelity is the breaking of trust that occurs when sexual and/or romantic secrets are deliberately kept from one's primary intimate partner.*

One of the reasons I like this definition is that it encompasses both online and real-world sexual activity. Furthermore, it is flexible depending on the couple. It allows couples to define their own version of sexual fidelity based on honest discussions and mutual decision-making. This means that it may be acceptable for one partner to look at porn (or to engage in some other extramarital sexual activity), so long as the other partner knows about the behavior and both are truly accepting of it. On the other hand, if one partner is looking at live webcam porn (or whatever) and lying about it or keeping the behavior secret, or the other partner doesn't find this behavior acceptable within the mutually agreed-upon boundaries of the relationship, then it qualifies as infidelity.

As a professional, I make no judgments about the ways in which couples mutually define relationship and sexual fidelity. In days of yore, marriage demanded a lifetime of mutual monogamy, but in today's world this is not always the case. The monogamy box is not for everyone. In fact, many couples, particularly younger couples, now seek "open" relationships with varying degrees of sexual freedom. As long as these healthy couples mutually agree, without manipulation or coercion, on the relationship boundaries, and so long as both parties then respect those boundaries, whatever they may be, and those boundaries don't diminish the couple's emotional bond, then it is not for me (or anyone else) to say that this is right or wrong.

That said, extramarital sexual activity, regardless of whether it reaches the level of sexual addiction, is typically not a mutually agreed-upon activity. More often, one partner values and upholds the couple's commitment to sexual fidelity (however that is defined) while the other does as he or she pleases and then hides their behavior, justifying it with endless variations of the following lies, ad nauseam:

- ✓ What my partner doesn't know can't hurt him/her.
- ✓ It's only online, so I'm not really cheating.
- ✓ Everybody does this. It's perfectly normal.
- ✓ We don't really have a sex life anyway, so this actually keeps us together.

Essentially, those who lie to their primary partners by living a separate sexual and/or romantic life convince themselves that what they are doing doesn't really count as a betrayal. Of course, that's not how their spouses and partners typically feel. For example, in our survey mentioned above, 87 percent of respondents said their partner's online sexual activity had an overall negative effect on their relationship, with 41 percent calling that negative effect "significant," and 35 percent saying it caused the demise of their relationship. The negative effects most commonly experienced by the cheated-on partners were loss of relationship trust, loss of self-esteem, stress, and anxiety brought on by the cumulative effect of the cheater's lying and secret-keeping, and diminishment of the sexual relationship. Consider the words of actual respondents:

- ✓ It obliterated the trust in our relationship. I no longer believe a single thing he says.
- ✓ We don't have sex often and it irritates me that he puts more time into the porn than trying to be intimate with me.
- ✓ I have been traumatized by the repeated discovery of his deception and betrayal of me with these activities.
- ✓ I became over-the-top with snooping, spying, trying to control the behavior, and thinking if I just did, then I could stop it. It caused complete erosion of my self-esteem, boundaries, and sense of self.
- ✓ Now I feel unattractive, ugly, wondering what's wrong with me. I can't sleep or concentrate. I'm missing out on life's happiness.
- ✓ My wife has cheated on me with a real partner, and it feels no different! The online "safe" cheating feels just as dirty and filthy as the "real-life" cheating.

Based on the results of our study, coupled with more than two decades of working with intimacy disorders, sex addiction, and couples battered by lies and infidelity, I can assure you that secretive online sexual activity is every bit as devastating as in-the-flesh cheating. In the eyes of the betrayed partner, there is no difference between digital dalliances and real-world affairs. Cheating is cheating. A lie is a lie, *even if it's a lie of omission*. Sexual infidelity destroys relationship trust, and learning about it and dealing with the outcome is painful, regardless of whether the infidelity occurred in person or online.

Understanding the Pain of Sexual Betrayal

As stated above, for spouses and partners of sex addicts it's not the extramarital sex that causes them the most pain. Instead, it's the betrayal of relationship trust: the lying, the secrets, and the ongoing deceit. For a healthy, emotionally attached primary partner this experience of profound and often unexpected betrayal can be incredibly traumatic. One study of women married to sexually addicted men found that many of these women, upon learning of their husbands' serial infidelity, experienced acute stress and anxiety symptoms characteristic of Post-Traumatic Stress Disorder.[2] To be clear, PTSD is not just experienced by soldiers who've survived active duty or victims of hurricanes and earthquakes. In reality, PTSD can be caused by any emotionally overwhelming experience—including serial relationship betrayals. Furthermore, it is a very serious anxiety-related illness, sometimes with life-threatening consequences. So the trauma of sexual infidelity, once found out, is severe.

The after-effects of spousal betrayal trauma most typically manifest in one or more of the following ways. It is important that both spouses and addicts see these (below) as a normal and healthy response to this type of emotional hurt, even though the behaviors and responses may seem "overwhelming" and "never-ending," leaving partners feeling like they will never be "themselves" again. Sadly, grief is grief, loss is loss, and, when directly related to profound emotional betrayal, can lead to emotional challenges like:

✓ Feelings of emotional instability, frequent mood shifts, "over-the-top" emotional reactions, tearfulness, rage, etc., sometimes actually followed by feelings of intense love, sexual desire, and a desire to "make it work"

✓ Hypervigilant behaviors (detective work), such as checking cellphone bills, wallets, computer files, phone apps, browser histories, and the like for evidence of infidelity both past and present

✓ Being easily triggered into mistrust of the cheating partner—trigger examples include the cheater coming home five minutes late, turning off the computer too quickly, looking "too long" at an attractive person, etc.

✓ Going on the attack by "lawyering up," spending money to punish the cheater, telling the kids age-inappropriate information about what the cheater did, etc.

✓ Telling children about the issues in detail, using them to side with a hurting parent against the addict.

✓ Having sex with others to "get even"

✓ Sleeplessness, nightmares, isolating, desiring to stay in bed and not "deal with the world"

✓ Difficulty focusing on day-to-day events, such as picking the kids up from school, work projects, maintaining a home, etc., without being distracted by intrusive thoughts or emotions

✓ Overcompensating by trying to lose weight, dress provocatively trying to be highly sexual in an attempt to "seduce" a spouse away from their addiction (which is not actually achievable, but can feel right in the moment)

✓ Obsessing about the betrayal and struggling to stay "in the moment," or alternately avoiding thinking about or discussing it.

✓ Escapist behaviors on the part of the betrayed spouse, both
   with substances (drugs and alcohol) as well as binge eating,
   spending, etc.

✓ Spending to get even

Sometimes there are gender differences in the way betrayed
spouses react after learning about their partners' sexual infidelity.
Generally speaking, betrayed females tend to see things globally,
thinking, "It's not just me that you've betrayed, it's also our kids, our
home, and our community." Women also tend to think, "If you lied
to me about this, then what else are you lying about? Can I believe
anything you've ever said?" Betrayed males, on the other hand, tend
to view spousal betrayal as a personal assault on their ego, thinking
things like, "Does this mean that I'm not a good enough husband
or lover?" or, even more narcissistically, "I can't believe you were out
there doing this while I was home trying to be a good husband. If I'd
known you were cheating, I would have been out there, too." But men
too can profoundly feel traumatized by a cheating spouse.

Regardless of gender, much of the trauma evoked by the disclosure of a supposedly monogamous sex-addict's behaviors stems from
timing. Sex addicts have obviously known about their extracurricular
sexual behaviors all along, and, once their behavior is discovered,
they often report feelings of relief that things are finally out in the
open. Betrayed partners, however, are typically blindsided and overwhelmed by this information. They're first learning about it, and
thus feel emotionally slammed by it. So while one partner may be
feeling relief, the other may feel as if he or she has been run over
by a Mack truck. Is it any wonder that betrayed spouses sometimes
respond in ways that make *them* look like the crazy ones? In reality,
survivors of this type of chronic betrayal trauma will very naturally
find themselves responding with rage, anger, fear, and/or any other

strong emotion. And this is to be expected, as they are not crazy; it's just that their whole world has been turned upside down.

Gaslighting Makes It Worse!

Gaslighting is a term that originated with the 1938 stage play, *Gaslight*, by British writer Patrick Hamilton. However, most people are familiar with the story through the Oscar-winning 1944 film of the same name, starring Charles Boyer and Ingrid Bergman. In the film, Boyer convinces his wife (Bergman) that she's imagining things, most notably the occasional dimming of the house's gas lights, as part of his plot to steal her deceased aunt's money and jewels. (The lights dim whenever he's in the attic, searching for the treasure.) Over time, Bergman comes to believe her husband's lies and, in turn, to question her sanity.

In today's world the plot of *Gaslight* seems pretty outlandish. Nevertheless, the concept of psychological abuse perpetrated by presenting false information and insisting those lies are true, thereby causing the victim to doubt his or her judgment, perception, memory, and even sanity, is relatively well-accepted in contemporary society—probably because gaslighting routinely occurs in conjunction with serial sexual infidelity and various forms of addiction.[3] Consider the words of Alexandria:

"DARREN WAS, AND SOMETIMES STILL IS, the most charming guy on the planet. We met at a party at a mutual friend's Manhattan penthouse. I was twenty-five, Darren was thirty. We've been dating for six years now, living together for five, and he keeps promising me we'll get married and start a family, but that never quite happens. The last three or four years, even though we're sharing an apartment, I almost never see him. He works in finance, and I know the hours are long, but sometimes I feel lonely and I try to call him but he doesn't answer his phone, even when he's gone all night or sometimes for an entire weekend. He doesn't even respond to my texts, just to let me know he's not dead.

"When he finally does show up, he tells me that his job is really demanding and I should cut him some slack. He'll tell me that he was working late on a really big deal which I should appreciate and not complain about, and he fell asleep at his desk, or he got called away to the country on short notice to meet with some hotshot client and didn't have time to let me know about it before he left, and then there wasn't cell service even though he tried to reach me. And then he reminds me that he's doing all of this for us, and that I really need to trust him because he loves me and would never do anything to hurt me, and if I really want to get married and have kids with him, then I have to stop acting crazy. And heaven forbid I accuse him of doing cocaine with his friends all night or sleeping with another woman. Then he calls me insecure and paranoid and all sorts of other things. Even though I have found evidence of both, recently. The worst part is that after a year or two of this I decided he must be right, that I really am crazy, jealous, and even paranoid about him/us.

"Last week he was gone for four days, and when he got back, he insisted that he'd told me over breakfast that he was going out of town on business. He said I was really groggy when he told me, so maybe it just slipped my mind. And I believed him! Then, yesterday, I went shopping a few minutes past noon and I walked past a café that we both like. There he was, sitting at a table for two with another woman, kissing passionately. Last night after he fell asleep I went through his iPhone and found out he's having affairs with *at least* three women! Now, instead of being mad, I feel crazier than ever. I can't eat, I can't sleep, I can't think straight, and I have absolutely no idea what to do next."

Alexandria presents a classic case of modern-day gaslighting. Essentially, Darren wanted to continue with his illicit sexual behavior so he crafted a web of lies to justify, deny, and cover up his activity. And when Alexandria had the good sense to question those lies, he flipped the script, insisting his falsehoods were true and that Alexandria was delusional or just making things up for some absurd reason. In this way, Alexandria was made to feel as if *she* was the problem, as if her emotional and psychological instability were the real issue.

The most disturbing thing about gaslighting is that even emotionally healthy people are vulnerable to it. In part, this is because we naturally tend to defend, excuse, and overlook concerns about the behavior of people to whom we are deeply attached. In larger part, it's because gaslighting starts slowly and builds gradually over time. In the beginning the lies are plausible, like, "I'm sorry I got home at midnight. I'm working on a very exciting project and I lost track of time." An excuse like that one sounds at least semi-reasonable to most people, and for a person who both loves *and trusts* the liar, it's easily accepted. Over time, however, as the cheating (or whatever else it is that the liar is trying to cover up) escalates, the fabrications also escalate. "I swear, I told you over breakfast that I was going away for four days. You must have forgotten." Most people would toss a lie like that one out with the garbage, but because the gaslighted partner has become inured to this type of deceit, even the most outlandish mistruths can be accepted. So instead of questioning the liar, gaslighting victims question themselves. In this respect, gaslighting is like placing a frog in a pot of warm water that is then set to boil. Because the temperature increases only gradually, the innocent frog never tries to jump out and save itself until it's too late.

Over time, gaslighting can result in what is known as a "stress pileup," leading to anxiety disorders, depression, shame, toxic self-image, and more, including, as mentioned above, symptoms

characteristic of Post-Traumatic Stress Disorder. Such is the abuse
that sex addicts intentionally perpetrate on their spouses and partners—all so they can continue their hidden sexual behaviors unabated.

Sadly, gaslighting behaviors are often more emotionally damaging
to a loving partner than whatever it is that the betrayer is attempting
to cover up. With Alexandria, for instance, the most painful part of
Darren's behavior wasn't that he was having sex with other women,
it's more about the way he lied about it ultimately leaving her feeling crazy and mistaken for doubting his many semi-plausible and/or
ultimately utterly outlandish excuses and fabrications.

Getting Help for Yourself

EMMA, A FORTY-NINE-YEAR-OLD LAWYER, learned about her
husband's sexual addiction five months ago. Upon learning about
his serial sexual infidelity, she got very angry and insisted that her
husband seek inpatient treatment for his issue, and that he follow up with ongoing outpatient therapy and regular attendance at
twelve-step sexual-recovery meetings. Initially, knowing that her
husband was in treatment—all the while watching him like a hawk
to make sure he wasn't slipping or relapsing—gave Emma a sense
of control, as did checking his email and cell phone daily. Eventually, though, she realized that her husband's treatment and recovery
wasn't enough to make her feel whole again. She says, "Somewhere
about six to seven months into the problem, I just got tired of the
whole thing being about him—his behavior, his emotional problems,
his shame and embarrassment, his consequences. What about me?
What about my pain and my fears about the future?" As Emma tired
of asking about her husband's therapy and worrying about whether
their relationship was going to survive, she found herself nagging and
becoming unnecessarily critical, letting her anger and frustration leak

out sideways in fits and starts. "Over time," she says, "as he slowly started to become more consistent and reliable (a good sign of his healing), I got less consistent and more unpleasant. *I started to really dislike the woman I was turning into.* That's when I finally sought help for myself."

As alluded to above, betrayed spouses and partners of sex addicts, despite the hurt, anger, confusion, and betrayal they experience, often resent the idea that they might need help to deal with their feelings and reactions. And this resistance is perfectly natural. After all, "he/she did this to me, to us, so why should I get help?" That said, many betrayed spouses do benefit from therapeutic assistance. At the very least they need to find validation for their feelings, education and support for moving forward, empathy for how their life has been disrupted by the addict's repeated betrayals, and help in processing the shame they feel about falling for all of the addict's now obvious lies and excuses. And if the relationship is ever going to truly move on, both spouses must be engaged in righting and steering that ship.

Six Do's and Six Don'ts

If you've learned about a partner's sexual infidelity, regardless of whether sexual addiction is in play, then you know the kind of pain we are talking about. It's not just the pain of any specific sexual betrayal that you must process and eventually overcome the big picture, it's the *loss of trust* in your spouse and your relationship that is really hard to take. Learning about a supposedly monogamous partner's extracurricular sexual activity near inevitably leaves you in a daze: stunned, hurt, uncertain, and unable to fully assimilate and accept what has happened. If you have recently learned about sexual addiction and/ or infidelity in your relationship and are experiencing any degree of anger, pain, and uncertainty, the following lists of do's and don'ts may be helpful.

Six things you *should do* if your partner is sexually addicted:

1) **Do get tested for STDs.** Men and women who engage in sexual infidelity are often careless about having protected sex (especially oral sex). It doesn't matter how much you love him or her or how much you want to believe that they wouldn't act in ways that might hurt you. As soon as you learn that your partner has been sexually unfaithful, you should visit your primary care physician, explain the situation, and ask for a full STD screen. If you don't feel comfortable going to a known doctor or clinic, seek out anonymous STD testing! Nearly every major metropolitan area in the US has such clinics or programs—just look online.

2) **Do investigate your legal rights, even if you plan to stay together.** Planning to stay together doesn't mean you will. Betrayed spouses should *always* find out their rights in a potential separation, including financial concerns, property concerns, and parenting issues if there are children. It is possible that your partner has already made plans to protect himself or herself legally and financially. You should do the same, regardless of what you hope the outcome of your situation will be.

3) **Do reach out to others for help.** Dealing with infidelity requires a level of emotional support that is beyond the life experience of most people, and the only healthy way to deal with this is to seek assistance from people who understand what you're going through: therapists, support groups like Al-Anon, S-Anon, CoDA, and COSA, along with trusted others who've dealt with similar betrayal, etc. Whether you decide to remain in the relationship or not, you need (and deserve) care,

love, and support, which can only be found by talking about what has happened with compassionate and empathetic others. You should not, however, be vindictive with this information. It's one thing to enlist others for support; it's quite another to tell your spouse's mother, children, boss, or best friend about his or her behavior out of spite. And keep in mind, *anything you say to your kids cannot ever be unsaid,* so think twice about bad-mouthing your fellow parent no matter how much you want to tell them.

4) **Do learn everything you can about sexual addiction.** This educational process helps you to better understand the sex addict, and also to make healthier decisions in the future.

5) **Do trust your feelings and observations.** If you don't feel safe with your partner, trust your intuition. If you don't see your partner getting ongoing help with his or her sexual problems—attending therapy and/or going to twelve-step support groups—then don't trust that things are getting better.

6) **Do expect to join your partner in therapy on your own and with your spouse if you want to work things out.** In therapy you may be able to request and receive a full accounting of your spouse's infidelity. If you are like most betrayed spouses and you don't want any more secrets in your relationship, then your partner, if he or she is also committed to salvaging the relationship, will, with the therapist's assistance, disclose what you want to know. This disclosure process best occurs in a therapy room, as the amount and nature of the information can be overwhelming. This process also calls upon the betrayed spouse to get ongoing therapeutic support to deal with information disclosed.

Six things you *should not do* if your partner is sexually addicted:

1) **Don't have unprotected sex with your partner.** No matter what a cheater tells you about his or her past sexual activity and/or recent STD tests, you absolutely should not have unprotected sex with that person until you feel confident that he or she has had a full (and clean) STD screen *and* that he or she has been faithful since being tested.

2) **Don't jump into long-term decisions early in the healing process.** This includes life-changing decisions such as whether to break up, file for divorce, leave with the kids, etc. The rule of thumb is *no major changes in the first six months of the recovery/ healing process.* That said, it's perfectly fine to sleep in different beds, to live apart while in therapy, and/or to limit your involvement in the relationship to what feels safe to you. Just don't make life-changing decisions when you are at the height of your pain, hurt, and anger unless you are committed to separation or divorce. If you are done, you're done, and that's okay, too. (see also #5 below)

3) **Don't try to use sex as a way to fix the problem.** While sexual intensity may feel good and intimate in the moment, using sex to assuage emotional pain is actually a form of mutual denial that moves you and your partner away from the process of healing.

4) **Don't go looking for sex outside the relationship as a way to get even.** "Revenge sex" may feel good in the moment, especially if your norm has been to feel neglected and unappreciated. But what may feel great for the few moments you're doing it might not feel right later, and will almost certainly cloud an already murky situation. Seeking sex as a way to manage hurt and resentment is a very poor choice, and it typically just makes things worse.

5) **Don't make threats you don't intend to carry out.** If you tell your partner that any further cheating will cause you to leave,

then you'd better pack your bags and go if/when he or she cheats again. Otherwise, you diminish your credibility. (It's usually best to not make threats at all. Say what you feel, but try not to make threats in the moment that you may regret later.)

6) **Don't stick your head in the sand or take blame for your partner's actions.** If you have an investment in your relationship, you can't avoid the hard facts of your partner's ongoing infidelity. Pretending the problem will go away will *definitely not* make it go away. Nor will blaming yourself. *Nothing that you did or did not do caused the infidelity.* Your partner had a choice. It doesn't matter how you've aged, how much weight you've gained or lost, or how involved you are with kids, family, friends, and/or work. There are many, much healthier ways that your partner could have expressed his or her unhappiness with you and/or aspects of your relationship than by doing this.

No matter what, relationship infidelity, especially when it's driven by sexual addiction, brings pain and heartache right along with it. And the worst thing you can do is to bottle things up and hope they'll just magically resolve. That just doesn't work. Instead, reach out for support, information, and advice—you deserve it. You will find many of the evaluational and support resources that will be useful to you in the Resources chapter at the end of this book.

Seeking Therapy

Typically, the best place for the betrayed partner of a sex addict to find treatment is with a licensed therapist who specializes in infidelity and related couples issues, perhaps someone who works in tandem with the addict's primary therapist. It is not recommended that betrayed spouses seek individual help from the same therapist as the addict, as this can result in "splitting" and "taking sides," which is unhealthy for everyone involved. Couples counseling is also recommended, although early couples therapy is usually more about venting and setting boundaries than it is about a couple's immediate healing. Sometimes, when both the addict and the betrayed spouse have primary therapists who specialize in sexual addiction, couples counseling can be a joint session with both therapists and both clients, rather than sessions with yet another clinician who specializes in couples work. In addition to being in therapy for themselves, betrayed partners should also expect to be aware of and even involved to some degree in the addict's treatment. In other words, a sex addict's recovery plans, friends, and healing process, etc. should not be a mystery to the cheated-on spouse, nor should that information be kept from them.

Over all, the primary initial concern in the treatment of a sexually betrayed spouse is safety. This includes physical health (STDs, family violence), emotional health, financial security, and child/family safety (young kids seeing Dad's porn, etc.). It is also important to uncover and process specific betrayals that might make the situation feel overwhelming, such as having an affair with a best friend or a relative.

It is always important for both partners to recognize and accept that the betrayed spouse is understandably riding an emotional rollercoaster, where feeling (and sometimes acting) crazy has become the new norm. In other words, the betrayed spouse is likely to display high levels of emotional lability (mood swings), and his or her own forms of acting out (raging, withdrawing, spending, eating, drinking, etc.) both in and out of the therapy room. Typically this lasts for as long as nine to eighteen months.

During this "crisis" period, the therapeutic needs of cheated-on spouses do NOT include:

- ✓ Attempts to calm them down
- ✓ Attempts to get them to look at "their part" in the relationship's problems
- ✓ Explorations of their childhood and/or their family history
- ✓ Explorations of their sexual/romantic life with their spouse
- ✓ Attempts to diagnose them as codependent, borderline, bipolar, or anything else, other than as a traumatized person in a state of shock who is grieving the damage to a relationship that he or she once held dear

Just as therapists would not diagnose the psychological makeup of parents coming to them for help after their child was hit by a car and seriously injured, therapists should not diagnose or label people coming for help after their lives have been flattened by the discovery of profound infidelity. Instead, therapists are best served by focusing on concrete ways to simply help that spouse get through the day. Prematurely forcing betrayed spouses to look at their own issues—any underlying psychological concerns that may (or may not) have led them into choosing and/or tolerating a cheating partner in the first place—typically just reinforces their feelings of being defective and/or at fault. As such, it is essential that therapists recognize the behaviors of betrayed spouses, however erratic they may appear, as nothing more than typical reactions to deep emotional trauma. (A year or so later, *after the crisis has abated, if the betrayed partner wishes it,* therapy can address any longer-term issues that he or she may have, such as childhood trauma, attachment deficits, low self-esteem, personality challenges, etc.)

Based on this information, for the first year or so of treatment (the crisis stage), the clinical needs of betrayed spouses and partners of sex addicts DO include:

✓ Concrete direction regarding healthcare issues, legal questions, and other forms of self-care

✓ Education about sexual addiction, trauma disclosure, and family dynamics

✓ Validation of the betrayed partner's intuition and feelings

✓ Assistance with full disclosure by the sex addict

✓ Guidance toward social support for what the betrayed spouse is experiencing (usually twelve-step based peer-support groups like Al-Anon, S-Anon, Codependents Anonymous, etc.)

✓ Insight into the effects of gaslighting on an intimate partner

✓ Structure geared toward moving forward

✓ Hope

Once again, betrayed spouses and partners of sex addicts have every right to feel angry, hurt, confused, and mistrustful. As such, they understandably rage, split, decompensate, do detective work, try to get an opinion from anyone they can find, and more. This is a healthy normal reaction to having your personal and family life shattered like a plate.

Getting Help for the Sex Addict

If you think your spouse may be a sex addict, usually the best thing you can do is to talk to him or her about it. Before doing this, though, you may want to take (or at least consider) the following steps:

✓ Talk to others who are close to your spouse to get their take on the situation. If you think it will help, you can try to develop an alliance of family, friends, clergy, and supportive others who can help you confront your partner.

✓ Gather as much factual information as you can about what your spouse is actually doing, and how it is affecting his or her life (and the lives of others, such as yourself).

✓ Consider how your partner is likely to respond to a confrontation. If you think a confrontation may be contentious, difficult, and possibly unproductive, consider hiring a professional interventionist (if you can afford it), as doing so increases your odds of success. (See the Resources chapter at the end of this book for more information on the intervention process.)

It is important to know, before you approach any sex addict, that confrontation is the absolute last thing the addict wants. Even sex addicts who know they have a serious problem will nearly always resist, lie, pretend, and cover up. Sadly, this is the face of their emotional/addictive disorder. However, if you truly care about this person, you will persist despite his or her resistance and potential anger.

When you are prepared emotionally and factually, the best way to confront a sex addict is to start by saying you are concerned about his or her sexual behaviors and well-being, and you think there might be a problem. Then you should list a few of the concrete, undeniable facts that are causing you to worry. Be as specific as possible with these facts, using "I" statements to reduce defensiveness on the part of the addict, such as:

✓ I worry because you stay up late on your computer every night, and whenever I wake up to go to the bathroom I catch you masturbating to porn or some person on a webcam.

✓ I'm afraid that we will lose our source of income because you've been warned twice by your job to stop using company-owned equipment for sexual purposes, but you continue to do it.

✓ I'm hurt, angry, and afraid because you contracted an STD and passed it along to me, and I wonder when it will happen again.

✓ I'm afraid that I will stop loving you if you don't get help.

After this, you should tell your spouse that you can no longer sit idly by while he or she ruins his or her (and your) life. Then you can offer to help your partner find books to read, sexual addiction treatment, and/or a twelve-step sexual recovery program. After that, it's pretty much up to the addict as to whether he or she wants to accept the help you've offered.

If you are worried that your partner may react violently to this type of intervention, do not attempt to undertake this process by yourself. If you are worried that you might be abandoned (including financially) if you undertake this process, you may want to first take steps that ensure your financial security and well-being *before* confronting your partner. Again, if you can afford it, you may want to consult an interventionist or knowledgeable addiction professional for advice and guidance.

With or without the assistance of a specialist, the end goals of the initial confrontation are the same:

✓ Let the sex addict know that you care about him or her.

✓ Let the sex addict know that you are worried (and why).

✓ Let the sex addict know that you will no longer co-sign or support his or her destructive sexual behaviors.

✓ Let the sex addict know that you hope he or she will accept the help you are offering.

It is important to remember throughout this process that *you cannot get well for another person*. Nor can you create in that person the motivation needed for recovery. The choice to get well or not is the addict's and nobody else's. No matter how badly you want this person to recover, no matter how great your love for this person, you can't magically make it happen. If and when the addict decides that he or she wants help, that help is available in abundance. But until that time the best that you can do is to voice your concerns and then refocus on caring about yourself.

If you find yourself struggling with this, you may wish to participate in Al-Anon, S-Anon, Codependents Anonymous, or similar faith-based or therapy support groups, where you will meet other concerned, loving people who are trying to live a healthy life while dealing with another person's infidelities and/or addictions. Sure, you may wonder why you're the one getting help when it's your partner who has the addiction, and this is a perfectly natural reaction. If and when you have it, remind yourself that you're in a difficult situation, even if you didn't cause it, and you deserve empathetic support and self-care regardless of what the addict does or does not do going forward.

Staying or Moving On?

When betrayed spouses choose to remain in their relationship, as they most often do, it can take a year or more of hard work on the part of both partners before they are able to reestablish any sense of meaningful, mutual trust. Rightfully so, too, after what they've been through. Happily, if the addict is committed to long-term behavioral change (sexual sobriety), living honestly, and regaining his or her personal integrity, the redevelopment of relationship trust is indeed possible. And when the betrayed partner joins the addict in his or her efforts at growth by also engaging in a process of support, education, and self-examination. The chances that the two will remain a couple over time nearly quadruples over couples where the addict alone gets help.

That said, some betrayed spouses of sex addicts do ultimately conclude that the violation they've experienced at the hands of the addict
is greater than their desire to remain in the relationship. For these
individuals trust cannot be restored, and ending the relationship may
be the best course of action. Just as a betrayed partner is not wrong to
continue a relationship with a sex addict, he or she is also not wrong
to end it.

Ultimately, more important than whether a betrayed spouse
chooses to stay or go is how he or she goes about growing beyond
the loss. This sort of recovery places a powerful emphasis on developing and trusting instincts, finding a greater willingness to express
emotions, engaging in self-care and self-nurture, and developing an
ongoing and trustworthy peer support network (via a therapy, twelve-
step or faith-based group).

13

Rebuilding Intimate Relationships

LISA, A THIRTY-SIX-YEAR-OLD college professor found out nine months earlier that her husband, Dan, was staying up late night after night, most often getting up after she had fallen asleep. Curious and concerned, she followed him one night to their home office, only to find her husband of nine years masturbating to porn and having webcam sex with other women in video chats. She sneaked out quietly, not telling him that she had been there or what she had seen. But the next morning before he left for work, she took a good look at his smartphone (thinking she might find some troubling emails), but instead what she spied there were multiple hook-up apps like Ashley Madison and Tinder that Dan had apparently been using to frequently facilitate casual sex during his workday.

Not surprisingly, this all blew up when they both got home from work that same day, and following several days of fighting, threats, and a lot of emotional handwringing on both sides, Dan finally agreed to seek treatment for his extensive patterns of sexual acting out. Concerned about her own emotional stability and the future, Lisa decided to enter therapy as well to help her work through what felt like, "a volcano of feelings erupting inside me."

Now, eleven months later, she says that her husband has been diligent about his recovery, even telling her about the one porn slip he had during that time. She is beginning to feel more hopeful now (where once she thought there was none) and is more optimistic about their potential future together and the chance that their relationship might truly survive. "I don't trust him completely yet (even though I want to), which under the circumstances feels quite healthy. Everyone in my women's support group agrees that this is normal and I am on the right track. I think that if he continues to be fully honest with me about what he is and is not doing my anger, even most of my distrust, will eventually go away. I'm also finally getting to the point where I can see that Dan didn't do this to me; he did it because he is a pretty broken guy. His behavior affected me, the family—everything— but I know that it is more about his internal struggles than about me or our relationship. That is a great relief to me on some level, though it took me a while to get there as I was so hurt and angry.

Restoring Trust

When sex addicts are in a relationship, that relationship has almost certainly suffered because of their addiction, even prior to any discovery. Typically, as discussed in the previous chapter, it's not the extramarital sexual activity itself that causes the most damage to the relationship, it's more over the *loss of trust* wrought by all the lies and secrets. In other words, what hurts committed partners the most is that their trust and belief in the person closest to them—the person with whom they are the most emotionally intimate—has been shattered. When this is the case in a sexually addictive relationship, then both partners, if they want to stay together, will need to find ways to nurture both themselves and their relationship, a process that starts with learning to trust once again.

One often difficult but rewarding step in this journey (for both the sex addict and the cheated-on spouse) is disclosure, which, as one might suspect, is a complete and thorough (but non-graphic) admission of the sex addict's behaviors, with the spouse and a professional (often more than one) present.

About Disclosure

This process should only occur with couples who've committed to remain together despite the addict's betrayals, and even then only when both parties have demonstrated a commitment to therapy and healing. In short, disclosure is a therapeutic process and, as such, it should not occur without the assistance of a sexual-addiction treatment specialist and/or a couples therapy specialist who can help both partners process and look beyond the pain of sexual betrayal. Whoever it is that oversees disclosure, the most important thing is for the sex addict to completely come clean,

Partial disclosure, followed by more partial disclosure at a later date, (voluntarily or if discovered), is a nightmare for spouses. The reason for this is simple: nearly all spouses want to regain trust, want to heal, and they often want the full truth in order to begin doing so. In this situation, half-truths held up for the spouse today as "this is everything you don't know" only to end up having more secrets revealed (or discovered) tomorrow evokes the opposite of trust, creating more suspicion anger and fear.

Helpful Advice for the Sex Addict

Recovering sex addicts, who have betrayed an intimate relationship, need to accept that they are *in the doghouse,* and rightfully so. If they want to save their relationship, they will need to earn back relationship trust, and this will not occur overnight. Whenever recovering sex addicts feel frustrated with their partner's (seemingly neverending) questions, anger, threats, mistrust, and demands, they need to remember that this is their own fault. They are the one who destroyed relationship trust. They are the one responsible for all of the pain. They are the one who made the choice to ignore vows of fidelity, to lie, and to keep secrets no matter their reasons. And if their cheated-on partner feels hurt by this and responds accordingly, for months upon months, so be it. In short, if recovering sex addicts want to save their relationships, they need to learn to be non-defensive and start accepting that until they behave differently—probably for quite some time—they may have to deal with hurtful, sometimes unwarranted unpleasant reactions from their spouse, and they need to be able to own that as a consequence of their lies and deceit. This doesn't mean that a sex addict is not worthy of caring support, it's just that at this time that help is not available, nor should it be expected to come from a betrayed spouse.

To facilitate the process of healing a damaged relationship, there are a number of attitudes that recovering sex addicts can adopt, and things that they can actively do, to show their spouse that they really do want to stay together and that they are willing to do whatever it takes to earn that privilege.

A few suggestions highly useful to implement include the following:

✓ Listen attentively to whatever your partner says. Try to hear what he or she is saying (both in and out of therapy) without reacting in a negative way. Breathe! Reach out for support. Try to see things from his or her perspective, keeping the pain of betrayal (caused by you!) in mind when you do so.

✓ Be grateful and humble that your partner hasn't left you, even though he or she is very angry. Remind both yourself and your partner that you are happy to be in this relationship, that you value it, and that you are sorry that you jeopardized it and them with your sexual addiction.

✓ When expressing yourself to your partner, don't expect him or her to "see your point" or to "understand" your reasoning. You need to remember that you've been lying to and keeping secrets from your partner for a long time, and the process of re-earning "the right to be heard" takes time.

✓ Don't expect a gold star for staying sexually sober or for simply being honest. Stopping your sexually addictive behaviors is the bare minimum you need to do if you want to save your relationship. It is not worthy of a pat on the back from your spouse. If you need positive reinforcement for little victories in recovery, seek them from your therapist, your twelve-step sponsor, and/ or friends in recovery, all of whom will cheer for you but not your spouse.

✓ Develop a pattern of honesty, not just with your spouse, but with everyone else in your life. If/when your spouse sees you being honest about difficult topics with others, he or she is more likely to believe that you're also being honest in your relationship and your recovery.

✓ Be patient. Don't expect everything to suddenly be okay overnight. Recovering from sexual addiction is a process. Rebuilding relationship trust is also a process. It is important to understand that your time frame and your spouse's time frame may be very different. Typically, rebuilding trust takes at least

a year. Until then, you just need to stick with the program and
wait things out.

✓ Understand that apologies are not enough. A thousand attempts
at "I'm sorry" are meaningless when compared to demonstrable
behavior change and a new pattern of truth. Besides, forgiveness
will not change your situation; you still have a lot of work to do.

✓ Understand that gift giving (even expensive gifts) is not that
useful here. Your partner wants honesty and relationship equal-
ity, not a bunch of stuff.

✓ Show your partner that you truly want to be with him or her
by spending time together, preferably doing things that he or
she enjoys, whether it's going to a movie, attending a gallery
opening, going to a ball game, working on the house, giving
them time to themselves, or whatever. It doesn't matter what
you do, as long as your partner sees that what matters to him or
her also matters to you. In other cases, some partners will also
need and request a lot of space, that the addict live elsewhere
temporarily, or take a "relationship" break. This is all reasonable
and understandable given the circumstances.

✓ Stay the course in your sexual recovery. If your sexual sobriety
goes away (relapse, not a slip), your relationship probably will
also. As such, it's important to establish and maintain a plan
for sexual sobriety, remaining committed to this plan no matter what.

The most important goal for recovering sex addicts is living a life
of rigorous honesty in all areas, small and large. It takes many days,
weeks, and months of consistency in this regard to overcome the
distrust they've created in the relationship. Simple things are very
meaningful when trying to reestablish trust. Knowing this, you may
want to consider the following:

✓ If you are going to be late, *even a little*, phone or text your partner to explain. If you agree to pick up some milk on the way home but forget, it is better to admit that you forgot than to make up some excuse (lying). And guess what, even when you tell the truth, thanks to all of your past lies and manipulations, your partner still may not believe you—*and you have to accept this.*

✓ If you need to use the computer or cell phone at home, it is better to do it in a high-traffic area than to sit behind a closed door expecting your partner to "just trust you" and to believe that nothing inappropriate is going on.

✓ Accept that your partner may (in the first sixty to ninety days or so) wish to GPS track your whereabouts, or have you check in by phone multiple times per day—and this is NORMAL for someone who is trying to restore trust after you've profoundly let them down.

✓ Willingly allow your partner to install filtering and accountability software on your computer, laptop, tablet, smartphone, and any other digital devices you use. This will not only help you to stay sober, it will help you to rebuild relationship trust.

✓ Let go of "winning," "being right" and "proving" anything to your spouse as this will only push them further away.

Helpful Advice for the Betrayed Partner

The work of saving a relationship damaged by sexual addiction does not fall entirely on the sex addict. Betrayed partners also have a role, which much of the time is about trying to make sense of how they feel about themselves in light of what has happened, while simultaneously becoming willing to (in time) trust the betrayer once again (or not).

If you are the betrayed spouse of a sex addict, there are several things you can do to help save your relationship. A few suggestions include:

- ✓ Educate yourself. The more you know about sexual addiction, early trauma, addiction in general, and things like co-addiction and enabling the better off you and your relationship will be.
- ✓ Commit to self-care. This includes your physical and your emotional needs. Try to eat right, get enough sleep, exercise, and maintain both your home and a social life. Also try to build and maintain a solid social support network. No matter what, don't let your partner's addiction and recovery become your sole focus. This is your time to heal.
- ✓ Try not to see your partner as the enemy. Most sex addicts are not bad people, even though they have behaved badly. And most often their bad behavior was driven, at least in part, by a combination of genetics and/or early-life trauma, both of which are factors beyond an addict's control. This doesn't mean you shouldn't allow all your feelings of hurt, rage, pain, and loss to come to the surface. Feel what you need to feel.
- ✓ If your partner is committed to a process of recognizing and overcoming his or her issues, try to view this as a positive—a growth opportunity for you both—rather than a negative.
- ✓ Be willing, over time, to grow beyond your anger about the betrayal and to find a pathway toward renewed trust and intimacy.
- ✓ Learn about forgiveness. Seriously, it is an actual science with some very readable books (see the Resources chapter) that speak to the stages and realities of forgiving.

What About Sex?

It is not unusual for one or both members of a committed couple to ask what to do about their sexual life together while in early recovery. While many spouses clearly state at the start that they wouldn't touch their loved one/addict with a ten-foot pole, moods change, hope can evoke warm feelings, and sometimes there you are—wanting to be sexual as a couple. The advice here is quite simple. Healthy couples have sex in part because they trust and love each other. While there may still be a great deal of love between an identified sex addict and their spouse in early recovery, it seems highly unlikely that there would be any degree of healthy trust. And rightfully so.

So here's the rub: why would you have sex with someone you don't trust? Those of us expert in these issues advise the following: it is highly useful for a couple who have just started dealing with these issues in an active way to take a time-out from sex in the first three to six months. Take the opportunity to work through the hurt, confusion, anger, and all the rest that needs work at the outset. Let yourselves get help and see how things evolve between you as that help is being obtained and new patterns between you are evolving.

Despite their often traumatized emotional state, some spouses may find themselves feeling more sexually attracted to the addict than in a long time, once they understand what has really been going on. For many spouses, the feeling of "finally being let in," while having long-held suspicions validated, can evoke long-distant feelings of closeness and hope. As one spouse put it, "Sex actually feels now like a safer and more interesting option than it has in a long time." Some spouses will want to have sex to reassure themselves that they are still attractive, that they are still "the one," or in an attempt to ward off feelings of abandonment and loss. Some will lose weight, buy sexy clothing and the like, all to encourage the addict to "spend all their sexual energy with them" as opposed to strangers or porn.

While all of the above are logical and reasonable responses to having sex, along with statements on both sides like, "We are a couple after all so what's the big deal" or "It's not like he or she is sexually acting out, we're married." Yet none of these responses acknowledges the reality that this couple is in crisis—may well be so for a year or more—and that *having sex (as much as it feels like it will) isn't going to solve anything*. Couples who are feeling close have many ways to express those feelings other than by having sex (genital, oral, or manual). This is a good time to focus more on caring interactions, both physical and emotional, rather than sexual. If you are feeling warm and loving toward your spouse, say it. If angry, tell them that, too. Intimacy is about being known and understood, not about looking good. Listening, helping out, a pat on the back, saying thank you, hugs: all small thoughtful acts that acknowledge, "Yes we are having a hard time, but we are still connected," can often go a lot further at this stage than a roll in the hay. Keep in mind that having sex is only one end goal of an intimate relationship—not a starter. Thus, having sex again (even in long-term couples) should not be taken lightly and is best discussed with supportive, safe, others (therapist, sponsor, clergy, close friend, etc.), before carried out.

To the Spouse: With sex with your mate off the table and as your mate is basically "in the doghouse" for a while, this can be "you" time. Go out and get a massage, take some yoga or meditation classes, take a night off each week to simply have fun with friends; you should have more free time now as this is time for the addict to take on more relationship responsibilities. This is the time for you to get back in touch with you: your body, your sense of what makes you happy, your friends and family, and, your spiritual life. Spouses, when not filled with anger and hurt, can well use this time to make themselves a priority, something that can often be neglected when living with an active addict.

To the Addict: Well, I guess this means that you won't be having sex for a while, and no, that won't cause you any physical harm or losses over time. You can wait a bit and while doing so this is a great time to note to yourself when you are feeling like having sex with your spouse (by not doing it), something you likely took for granted in the past. As busy as you will be with support groups, therapy, reading, writing, and the like, this is also a time for you to build emotional intimacy with your spouse in many of the ways described above and more. You, too, need to have some fun (nonsexual), work on safe friendships and take this time out to learn more about yourself, rather than focusing on, "When will I get to have sex again?" Sex will be there when you are ready; in the meantime you can work at becoming a better person while on this temporary "time out."

Note to Both: This is not a punishment, it is an opportunity. It is an exercise in self-restraint, self and other respect, and a time to match-up your emotional and sexual lives together, something often out of whack during active addiction. Make-up sex won't help with problems this big, but it *can* make things *worse*. But having sex when you are ready, when it feels right and when others working with you agree that you are both ready—well that can bring you more safety and connection (both individually and as couple) than you likely expected or even have experienced in the recent past.

Helpful Advice for the Couple

Couples working to overcome sexual addiction often find this process difficult and rocky. As stated early on, the addict and the betrayed partner are often in very different places emotionally and psychologically.

Couples hoping to salvage a damaged relationship need to be patient, allowing one another to feel and express whatever is true for them in the moment, even if that particular stage of the process is unpleasant for one or both parties. At all times, both individuals need to be honest about what they are thinking, feeling, and experiencing. Furthermore, both parties need to understand that the relationship—after all of the damage wrought by the sex addict's behaviors, lies, and secret-keeping—will never go back to the way it was. It may eventually be just as good or even better (or maybe not), but it won't ever be the same.

Sometimes a structured setting or structured activities can help a couple "come together" again in ways that rebuild the relationship. These may be fun things, or they might be therapeutic in nature. A few possible ideas include (but are not even remotely limited to) the following:

- ✓ Going to couples counseling
- ✓ Attending twelve-step recovery meetings together (at Recovering Couples Anonymous, for instance)
- ✓ Planning family activities
- ✓ Taking romantic (though maybe nonsexual, especially early in the recovery process) getaways
- ✓ Scheduling dates, and keeping them no matter what
- ✓ Setting aside time each day to listen, really listen, to one another
- ✓ Doing chores together (grocery store, yard work, cleaning house, etc.)
- ✓ Starting a social media page together
- ✓ Volunteering together at a local charity
- ✓ Seeking out recommended weekend couples' intensives or workshops, using those experiences to further grow together and separately.

Once the initial wave of confusion, pain and secrecy has passed (a period that often requires a more individual than couples focus), the more time couples dealing with sexual addiction spend together, the better. But this time should not be entirely focused on the addiction and/or recovering from the addiction. Just as the addict needs to live in his or her "outer boundary," so does the couple, and this means having fun together in addition to the drudge work of recovery.

14

Long-Term Healing

JAMIE, A SINGLE, THIRTY-THREE-YEAR-OLD chiropractor now in sexual recovery for almost two years, has gained significant clarity about his addiction. He says, "My cyber-sex problems didn't come just because I had a laptop and an iPhone. I see now that I had issues with sex long before I discovered webcams and hookup apps. But once I got online, it got out of hand pretty quickly because suddenly I had access to the world's biggest singles bar. Unfortunately, I got so caught up in my online fantasies that I slowly lost focus in things like my job, my friends, my family, and taking care of myself in general. Basically, my life came apart at the seams and I didn't really see how bad it was until my brother and sister stepped in and forced me to get help. At first I was really angry with them, but now I feel incredibly grateful that they did this. Today I have a new job, a really nice apartment, and I've started dating. I haven't found the right person yet, but that's okay because I'm probably not ready for a long-term relationship anyway. But I will be someday, thanks to my recovery, and I'm really looking forward to that.

For most sex addicts in the process of healing, sexual recovery has distinct stages that are moved through in fits and starts. For instance, in the first few weeks and months of healing, sex addicts are typically focused on the basic steps of separating themselves from both their denial and problematic behaviors, defining what sexual sobriety means for them, developing and implementing a personalized sexual boundary plan, and finding useful therapeutic assistance. As recovery progresses and sex addicts become more comfortable living within the bounds of their personalized plan for sexual recovery, things like friendships and romantic relationships become more important.

As discussed throughout this book, sexual addiction, at its core, is little more than a maladaptive attempt to simply feel okay in an individual who struggles with shame, self-esteem, intimacy, and emotional self-regulation. When viewed this way, it is easy to understand that long-term recovery must address these issues in meaningful ways. In other words, the keys to lasting sexual sobriety lie beyond the formation of a sexual boundary plan. Long-term healing is a lot about creating and deepening the kinds of the relationships required for long-term accountability. As such, sex addicts who truly desire long-term sexual sobriety and a better life will agree to be fully honest with and take advice from other people. Sometimes they may be asked to implement constraints that irk them, that they may not see a need for, and becoming accountable for their actions to people they barely even know, all because *they truly wish to heal* from their addiction.

The good news is that even those who are merely going through the motions of sexual sobriety to appease others—a spouse, a boss, legal authorities, etc.—can benefit from the early machinations of recovery. Even if they continue to act out in secret, as many of these individuals choose to do, they still, at the very least, become aware that active sexual addiction becomes harder and harder to conceal, and that living a double life grows ever more stressful. They also tend to see that over time compulsive sexual behavior becomes less and less enjoyable, and less and less effective as a means of emotional self-soothing.

In Alcoholics Anonymous they sometimes say that nothing is worse than a belly full of booze and a head full of recovery. This is also true with sexual addiction. Once the addict knows that he or she has a problem, compulsive sexual behaviors lose their appeal. As soon as the addict's denial begins to crack, sexually addictive behaviors can never again occur without at least a tiny understanding that "this is a very bad idea and I really need to stop."

Eventually, of course, sex addicts must fully commit to a recovery process (like it or not) or they will continue sliding into the ever-deepening downward spiral of their addiction. Those who opt for the former nearly always find that by taking steady steps forward, their lives steadily get better. And those who opt for the latter nearly always experience a continuing and ever-escalating series of negative life consequences. If they are lucky, they may eventually return to the recovery and healing process with a true commitment to change.

Progress, Not Perfection:
Understanding Slips and Relapse

JONATHAN, A FORTY-NINE-YEAR-OLD CHEMIST, entered outpatient treatment and twelve-step recovery for sexual addiction after more than a decade of sexual acting out left him emotionally exhausted and borderline suicidal. In the beginning, he attended individual and group therapy every week, never missing a session, and twelve-step meetings on the days he was not in treatment. In addition to completing his therapy assignments and starting to work the twelve steps with his Sex Addicts Anonymous (SAA) sponsor, he began to journal pray and meditate on a regular basis. Over time, he started to view his sexual acting out as a symptom of a difficult time in his life that was now past, rather than something that he needed to deal with on a daily basis. After nine months away from compulsive sexual behaviors, he started to ease up on his program of recovery, not going to twelve-step meetings as often, skipping therapy sessions, and choosing not to check in with his sponsor when he was supposed to. Finally, one Saturday after a hectic workweek, he thought, *I should really just relax today and take some time for me. I deserve it.* So instead of going to his Saturday morning SAA meeting, he slept in. And when he finally rolled out of bed, he decided to go online just to "prove to himself" that he had things under control. Within minutes, he'd arranged to meet a stranger for sex.

What Went Wrong?

Sadly, slips and relapses are common, almost expected, in early recovery from sexual addiction. As such, it is important for sex addicts (and their loved ones) in the process of healing to understand that temporarily backsliding into the psychological pull of addiction, as Jonathan did, is not the end of the world, nor does it mean they've failed. Instead, it is a learning opportunity and a chance to reaffirm and hopefully strengthen their commitment to living differently in the future. Yes, some sex addicts are lucky. They create their boundary plans and stick to them right from the start. However, most experience at least a few bumps in the road, slipping or relapsing at least once or twice. Something no spouse ever wants to hear or accept, but nonetheless is important to acknowledge and accept provided the addict remains honest about their struggles. Either way, *the process of recovery and healing is about progress rather than perfection.* No addict ever recovers perfectly, nor should any sex addict ever expect to do so. Note that this statement *is not* an excuse to slip.

Sex addicts should also be aware that slips and relapses are not the same thing. Let's take a look at the differences here:

Slip: This is a brief, mostly unintended return to addiction. Sometimes an unexpected stressor or a poorly constructed sexual-boundary plan that leads toward and not away from triggers can lead to a slip. A slip can be managed and contained by immediate and honest disclosure. After a slip, recovering sex addicts *must* tell others—therapists, twelve-step sponsors, accountability partners, spouses, and supportive friends in recovery (including their spouses!)—about the event if they hope to get back on track. Like it or not, *honesty is absolutely* key here to prevent progression of the disorder!

Relapse: By definition, a relapse is a series of slips that occur one after another, most often because an addict keeps that first one secret, choosing to minimize, rationalize, hide and/or justify his or her behavior over integrity and honesty. Their secrets and hiding then set the stage for a full range of relapse behaviors to occur with increasing frequency and intensity. Before long the addict is back where he or she started: struggling with full-blown, out-of-control sexual addiction.

Common warning signs for slips and relapse include:

✓ **Overconfidence:** "This is going really well. Maybe I have the problem licked."

✓ **Denial:** "See, I can stop my sexual acting out without any trouble. Now that I've proved this, I can look at porn like a normal person, without worrying about consequences."

✓ **Isolation:** "I can handle this on my own. I don't need to go to therapy or twelve-step meetings, and I don't need to be in constant contact with other recovering sex addicts."

✓ **Blaming:** "If my spouse hadn't gotten that new job that takes up so much of his/her time and energy, I wouldn't feel like I need to go online to socialize."

✓ **Making Excuses:** "I know that being alone with my computer is a danger zone, but I need to stay late at the office to finish this important project."

✓ **Setting Up Slippery Situations:** "The buffet at that Chinese restaurant across the street from where the prostitutes hang out is really good, so I'm going to have lunch there alone today."

✓ **Minimizing:** "I'm only looking at a little porn. It's not like I've gone back to having affairs with real people."

✓ **Ignoring or Devaluing Feedback from Supportive Others:** "The people in my therapy group and my twelve-step group just want to control me. The stuff they want me to do might work for them, but they really don't understand me and my situation."

✓ **Feeling Victimized:** "I don't understand why I have to deprive myself when everybody else can look at porn and have webcam sex without fear or problems."

✓ **Rationalizing:** "It's okay for me to 'step out' when I'm traveling for work or on vacation. My 'rules for sobriety' don't count when I'm in a different state and besides, no one will know."

✓ **Ignoring Previously Agreed-Upon Guidelines:** "I know that I promised my wife I wouldn't look at porn or flirt with other women on hookup apps, but what she doesn't know can't hurt her."

✓ **Feeling Entitled:** "I've worked really hard in my recovery for six months, and I've been pulling double duty at work, and nobody seems to appreciate the effort I'm putting in. I deserve a little something just for me."

As mentioned above, slips and relapse are not the end of the world, though they often feel like failures and feel shameful to discuss. Rather than looking at these events as disasters with no solution, recovering sex addicts (and their support networks) should view them as the growth opportunities that they truly are. In other words, setbacks should be treated as problems to be explored and solved rather than personal failures. As such, after a slip or relapse, addicts, working with knowledgeable others, can (step by step) explore the "stinking thinking" that led to their backslide, identify the trigger or triggers that pushed them over the edge, and devise ways in which they can handle themselves differently in the future if the same or a similar situation arises. They should also explore other situations in which they might relapse, planning for ways to cope there as well. If necessary, they can tighten up their sexual boundary plan.

> Though slips and relapse are quite common in the early stage of sexual recovery, this does not mean that sex addicts should feel that they have permission to go ahead and slip. And even though sex addicts should not emotionally attack themselves after a slip, they will need to have empathy for a spouse who's been betrayed by them yet again and is now quite angry.

No matter what, any recovering addict who finds himself or herself in the midst of a slip or relapse should immediately get honest about what's going on, confessing to his or her therapist, spouse, twelve-step sponsor, and social support group. Recovering sex addicts establish these loving and empathetic connections for a reason; now is the time to use them. If a sex addict in the midst of a slip or relapse is unable or unwilling to ask for help, and full own up to their challenges, his or her downward slide will almost certainly continue. If, however, that person reaches out and asks for assistance, he or she can save his or her sexual sobriety, along with the good life that accompanies it.

Basic Tools of Sexual Recovery
(i.e., Coping Mechanisms)

Unfortunately for sex addicts, sexual triggers are unavoidable, as sex is so thoroughly baked into our consumer culture. In today's world, anyone, anywhere, anytime can be triggered into sexual desire: driving past one sexy billboard after another, seeing someone showing just a bit too much skin at the mall, sitting in the stands at a kid's soccer match, picking up a magazine at a friend's house, hanging out at a neighborhood party, attending a work event, taking the dog for a walk, going to the movies, working out, sitting at home watching TV, picking up a cell phone, driving through a particular neighborhood, etc. Triggers are endless in number and variety, and there is quite literally nothing to be done about this beyond *learning what it feels like* to be triggered and how to *implement healthier (i.e., nonaddictive) coping* choices when needed.

When sex addicts are triggered, it is important that they have a "recovery toolbox" that they can reach into in their moment of crisis. After all, utilizing one or more healthy coping mechanisms (tools of recovery) is the only consistently effective way to short-circuit the addictive cycle. A few essential tools for recovering sex addicts include (but are not even remotely limited to) the following:

✓ **Utilizing a Recovery or Accountability Partner:** Addiction is best chased into remission by honesty, vulnerability, and transparency with another person who is aware of the problem and utilized as a sounding board, support person, co-decision-maker (around sexual and romantic choices), etc. To go it alone most often means remaining addicted or trading one addiction for another. It takes practice and hard work to consistently reach out to another person for direction, especially when related to sexual decision-making (private, personal etc.). But it must be done and with the right person; someone who is non-shaming, but unafraid to give unfiltered, honest feedback. Addicts are far too good at convincing themselves that things are "okay" whereas a neutral, caring outsider would clearly not see them as "okay." Therapists, sponsors, long-term friends, and clergy often can serve in this role. As stated, it is best to not give this task to a spouse or romantic partner, as they are too personally involved to be neutral and nonjudgmental when giving direction and advice.

✓ **The Sexual Boundary Plan:** Sexual boundary plans are created for several reasons—helping addicts to understand the nature of their addiction and to define their personal version of sexual sobriety, identifying "slippery" areas to watch out for, and providing addicts with guidance when they are triggered and unsure of what to do next. Many sex addicts carry printed or digitized versions of their boundary plan with them at all times. That way, if/when addicts feel triggered, they can look at their inner boundary and see that a particular behavior is prohibited. More important, they can look at the outer boundary and find a handy list of alternative activities. For most sex addicts, even a quick glance at certain outer boundary items—"re-earn the respect and trust of my wife and kids," for instance—is enough to halt the addictive cycle.

✓ **Twelve-Step Sexual Recovery Meetings:** To maintain long-term recovery, sex addicts need places where they can talk openly and honestly, without fear of judgment, about their addiction, including when, where, why, and how they are sometimes triggered. This is doubly true after they've been triggered and then struggled to halt the addictive cycle. By far, the most readily available safe (empathetic, nonjudgmental, and relatively private) place to do this is before, during, and/or after group therapy and/or a twelve-step sexual recovery meeting. Put simply, *one of the most powerful tools in the box is talking to another recovering sex addict.* And if no meeting is taking place at that moment, addicts can turn to their group's phone list and call anyone on it. Having this handy list of phone numbers of supportive friends in recovery is essential when addicts have an urge to act out, when they need immediate help in a crisis, or when they simply want support and guidance from someone who "speaks their language."

✓ **HALT:** This is an acronym for Hungry, Angry, Lonely, and Tired. Any of these simple conditions can leave an addict more vulnerable than usual to acting out. Let's face it, even healthy, non-addicted people tend to behave in ways they might later regret when their judgment is clouded by hunger, anger, loneliness, or exhaustion. The trick here is for addicts to recognize and address these needs when they arise, rather than simply lumping them in with every other form of emotional discomfort that they don't want to experience (and once tried to avoid by acting out sexually). As such, especially when triggered in early recovery, sex addicts must learn to HALT and ask themselves: When is the last time I ate? Did I get enough sleep last night? Is there some conflict in my life that I need to resolve? Would a few minutes spent talking with someone who understands me help me feel better? More often than not, a catnap, a candy bar, or a five minute phone conversation will greatly diminish the desire to sexually act out.

✓ **Self-Care:** It can be difficult to think of someone who is having a great deal of sex as being "deprived." But it is a fact that most active addicts of all stripes can and will ignore even their most basic physical needs (eating, sleeping, daily showers, etc.) in order to remain engaged in their addiction of choice. Thus a defined routine of self-care that is inclusive of diet, exercise, medical check-ups, recreation, and fun (alone and with others) are as important to keeping an addiction in check as are all the don'ts and don'ts and can'ts that are in place to discourage problem behavior.

✓ **"Bookending" Difficult Events:** Sometimes sex addicts are triggered unexpectedly. Other times, triggers can be anticipated long in advance. For instance, attending a social engagement where people will be looking their best and drinking alcohol is an obvious potential trigger for most sex addicts. Knowing this, addicts can arrange to "bookend" such an event with phone calls to their therapist, twelve-step sponsor, accountability partner, and/or another supportive person in recovery. During the "before" call, an addict commits to sobriety, and he or she may even discuss plans to avoid relapse in this particular situation. The "after" call provides an opportunity to discuss what happened, what feelings came up, and what the addict might need to do differently next time. (The practice of bookending also helps with the "lonely" portion of HALT.)

✓ **Practicing Gratitude:** Sex addicts have typically used their sexual fantasies and behaviors to numb themselves for so long that they've forgotten how to experience emotions—especially uncomfortable ones like anxiety, depression, shame, fear, and the like—in a healthy way. Sometimes, especially early in the recovery process, sex addicts can become overwhelmed by those feelings and lose sight of what is going right in their lives. A great way to combat this is to create a gratitude list. Writing a ten-item gratitude list nearly always counteracts almost any trigger and halts the addictive cycle. For some sex addicts, every gratitude list begins the same way: "I am grateful to be sober at this moment." A side benefit of gratitude is that it promotes happiness. As my colleague Brené Brown notes in her book, *Daring Greatly*, gratitude and joy are inextricably linked.[1] After conducting quite literally thousands of in-depth interviews examining the causes and underlying factors of happiness, Dr. Brown found one primary difference between happy people and unhappy people: happy people are grateful for what they have. Period. People who are grateful for what they have tend to focus on their strengths rather than their weaknesses, and they are in general more hopeful, less stressed-out, less likely to wallow in shame and depression, and *more likely to recover from an addiction.*

The Three-Second Rule

Sex addicts (just like the rest of us) are not in control of the thoughts and ideas that pop into their minds at any given moment. What they can control, however, is how they act when they unexpectedly encounter problematic thoughts, triggers, or ideas. For instance, after recognizing that there is an unexpectedly attractive or seductively dressed person on the street, for example, they can train themselves to do the following, rather than allowing themselves to "get into" addiction thinking (try it, it works well).

1st Second—Take one second to acknowledge that this is an attractive person or situation that you find arousing and a turn on (sexual attraction is a natural part of being human that must be acknowledged, not shamed or avoided).

2nd Second—*Look away.* Look down or away, take this second to appreciate the sky, your surroundings, anything other than the object of your desire. Let yourself be aware that you are struggling; that you would rather keep staring at that person or get something (sexual) going with them or someone else. Allow the feeling, but instead of acting on it, take an opposite action by choosing to look away.

3rd Second—While still looking away, imagine in your mind that person as someone's daughter, granddaughter, nephew, son, etc. See them (in your mind, not by looking at them a second time) as a genuine, spiritual, real person, worthy of love, who doesn't deserve to be used sexually or romantically and then thrown away.

Then keep moving on. By allowing the feeling, choosing to turn away and then de-objectifying the person, you get to stay in the world and feel okay about yourself, as a healthy person with healthy sexual desires, who does not act on them every time you feel them, and as someone who appreciates that people are people, not objects. The more addicts practice this simple exercise the easier it becomes to "be" in the world with less temptation and more hope.

Obviously, the half-dozen tools listed above are hardly the full kit. Journaling, written twelve-step work, ongoing outreach to others in recovery, twelve-step sponsorship (both giving and receiving), reading recovery-related literature, changing old routines, developing healthy hobbies, prayer, meditation, and just plain "thinking it through" are just a few of the hundreds of other tools that sex addicts can use to combat their addictive patterns.

Before proceeding, I'd like to pause and reiterate one particularly powerful statement from the above information: when sex addicts are triggered, the most powerful tool they have is their willingness to let another recovering pre-designated, caring, non-judgemental person know that they are struggling. As such, the sex addicts who do best in recovery are those who are willing to throw themselves wholeheartedly into seeking out and finding a healing community (twelve-step, faith-based, group therapy, etc.) making friends, making and taking recovery-related phone calls, fully engaging in their twelve-step meetings, and/ or other support groups, and willingly being of service to others.

The "Recovery Value" of Guilt and Shame

HARVEY, A FORTY-YEAR-OLD, SOON-TO-BE DIVORCED father of one, struggles with pornography, hookup apps, and prostitutes. Six months ago, Harvey contracted an STD, which he then passed to his wife. That's how she found out about his behaviors. But even that didn't stop him. And after his wife moved out, taking their daughter with her, Harvey's behavior escalated even further to the point of his feeling suicidal. Now in treatment, he says, "I see that when my sexual problems started to take off I felt bad about what I was doing, but I still thought I was a decent person. As my behaviors progressed, though, my perception of myself changed. By the time I found out that I had given my wife a disease, I honestly felt like I was a bad person so there was no point in trying to change. I thought I deserved all the punishment and misery I was about to experience, and that belief made it easier for me to just keep digging a deeper hole." Now that Harvey is several months sober, he is working on his self-image in addition to containing his sexual behaviors.

Sadly, sex addicts often feel shame (about who they are), rather than guilt (about what they have done). Meaning that they feel as if something within themselves is the cause and crux of their problem, as if they are flawed in some deeply meaningful way and therefore doomed to a life of misery, isolation, and regrettable behaviors. Oftentimes sex addicts in the process of healing need a great deal of time before they can even begin to understand that they are not inherently defective, that it was their maladaptive choices and not their true selves that caused their addiction and its related negative consequences. Time is also needed for them to gain insight and empathy into the pain they have caused others. The good news is that once recovering addicts finally begin to understand that they are good people who've behaved badly, rather than bad people who are just doing what bad people do, the process of healing begins to accelerate.

Angry Spouses

Even though a recovering sex addict may be working very hard in therapy and twelve-step recovery to overcome his or her shame and to feel better about who he or she is as a person, this work may not feel reinforced or even supported by an angry, betrayed spouse. Instead, the cheated-on spouse may frequently accuse the addict of "ruining our lives" and of being a horrible person. And understandably so, after all that the addict has done, even the most empathetic, loving spouse can be very hurt and angry for a long time. This is why recovering sex addicts need a larger support network—people who understand the true nature and causes of sexual addiction, as well as the process of recovery. After all, if the only messages an addict receives are shaming, then the addict will never be able to overcome his or her shame-based sense of self.

It is important to note, once again, that guilt and shame are very different, especially from the standpoint of recovery and healing. In fact, when a sex addict experiences guilt (rather than shame) after violating his or her core values—especially when the behavior has harmed not only the addict but other people—it shows that the addict does indeed have a moral compass. Even better, the supposedly negative emotion of guilt can be a catalyst for long-term behavior change and lasting sexual sobriety. Essentially, the desire to not experience the emotional pain wrought by guilt healthfully encourages all of us to not repeat past mistakes, while also helping us develop empathy for others and a desire to make amends to those who've been harmed.

Unfortunately, many sex addicts live with profound internalized feelings of shame and self-loathing that are tied more to their inherent sense of self than to any specific activities or behaviors. These individuals often feel like bad, unlovable people, and that their problematic sexual behavior simply serves as proof of this fact. When this occurs, a phenomenon generally referred to as a *shame spiral* or *narcissistic withdrawal* prevents sex addicts from seeing past their self loathing, thereby pulling them further into depression and isolation—both of which are serious obstacles to healing.

The prevalence of shame spirals among sex addicts is one of the (many) reasons that social support is such an important element of the healing process. Put simply, shame does not occur in a vacuum. Instead, it occurs between people, and it therefore heals best between people. In fact, numerous studies have shown that *discussing a traumatic/shaming event with a supportive person or people greatly reduces its short- and long-term negative effects.*[2] Dr. John Briere, a long-time leader in the field of trauma/shame research and treatment, has consistently stressed that it is not any specific traumatic event that causes the most stress and damage, it's how that event is handled within the family/community.[3] Dr. Briere and many other clinicians have found that when traumatized and shamed people share their most difficult experiences—the events that leave them feeling defective, unworthy, and unlovable—even long after the fact, their stress levels decrease, and their overall mental and physical health improves.[4]

Of course, sharing about traumatic events and deep shame is, by nature, incredibly painful. As such, most people would "rather eat dirt" than talk about this stuff. Nevertheless, it is clear that shame, self-hatred, and self-loathing thrive in darkness but wither in sunlight. In other words, the best way to reduce the power of a shame-based self-image is to talk about shameful feelings and events with safe, supportive, empathetic others: the kinds of people that recovering sex addicts routinely encounter in sex-addiction-focused group therapy faith based and twelve-step sexual recovery groups.

15

Final Thoughts

For most of us, sexual fantasies and behaviors are one of many pathways to enjoyment, play, and intimate connection. However, sexual addicts use these activities compulsively, finding over time that they've lost control and must deal with negative life consequences as a result. Their belief systems, their self-esteem, and their relationships suffer, all thanks to their addiction. Happily, the definition of sexual sobriety does not include total abstinence. Instead, sex addicts must, like people who struggle with eating disorders, find a way to healthfully integrate this naturally important element of life into their day-to-day existence. This book provides sexual addicts (and those who care about them) with a road map for doing this.

Over the last several decades, countless thousands of sex addicts and their loved ones have found recovery and healing by following the steps outlined herein: understanding and recognizing their problem, visiting a knowledgeable sex-addiction treatment specialist, getting involved in twelve-step and/or related support groups, dealing with concurrent disorders related to their addiction, setting appropriate boundaries for sex, dating, and relationship integrity, rebuilding their relationships, and restoring balance and freedom to their lives. And the best news of all is that it's incredibly easy to get started. All that is needed is a willingness to be honest and to openly begin seeking help.

If you are sexually addicted, or you think that someone you know and care about is sexually addicted, I hope you have found this book both enlightening and helpful, and that you feel motivated to undertake the process of recovery, healing, and a more meaningful, connected and rewarding life. If so, everything you need to get well is out there waiting for you to get started. I wish you all the best in your journey.

16

Recovery Resources, Support, and Education

Features to Look for in Filtering and Monitoring (Parental Control) Software Products

As mentioned repeatedly throughout this book, modern-day sexual addiction is a digitally driven endeavor. A decade or so ago, it was reasonable to suggest to sex addicts that they either stay away from computers altogether, or use them only in very limited circumstances. But that was then and this is now. In today's world, digital technology is an increasingly essential part of healthy human interaction and connection, and the vast majority of recovering sex addicts can't simply abstain or even significantly limit their use of it. The good news is that sex addicts can now fight fire with fire, installing "parental-control software" on their digital devices.

As the parental-control label suggests, these products were initially developed to protect children from unwanted online content and contacts. However, as the products have become more sophisticated over time, they have also become more versatile, and many are now quite useful to adults who struggle with online behaviors, including sexual behaviors.

Generally speaking, parental-control software products offer a combination of filtering/blocking and monitoring/accountability. The filtering portions of these programs offer variations of the following:

- ✓ Customizable website filtering and blocking
- ✓ Online search filtering and blocking
- ✓ App filtering and blocking
- ✓ Social media blocking
- ✓ Instant message/chat blocking
- ✓ File transfer blocking (preventing the sending and/or receiving of pictures, videos, and the like)
- ✓ Video game filtering
- ✓ Profanity blocking

The accountability features of these products typically include variations of the following:

- ✓ Regular and on-demand reports (for the accountability partner)
- ✓ Real-time alerts if the sex addict uses or attempts to use a digital device in a prohibited way
- ✓ Log of websites visited
- ✓ Log of online searches
- ✓ Log of social networking sites utilized

✓ Log of usernames and passwords

✓ Log and/or transcript of IM and chat activity

✓ Log and/or transcript of email activity

✓ Screenshot playbacks

It is important to state that filtering and accountability products are not guarantees of sexual sobriety. In truth, a persistent and/or tech-savvy sex addict can nearly always find ways to circumvent even the best of these products. And if an addict is stumped by the software, he or she can just go out and buy a new digital device and then use it in secret. As such, filtering and accountability products should not be viewed as *enforcers* of recovery; instead they should be looked at as *a tool* of recovery that can help sex addicts maintain sobriety by reducing impulsive online behavior (through the filtering and blocking features), and rebuild trust (through the accountability and reporting features). Unsurprisingly, some of these products are better than others; annually updated reviews are posted on the website of the Sexual Recovery Institute at: *sexualrecovery.com/online -controls-for-sex-romance-addicts/*.

Twelve-Step Sexual Recovery Groups Q&A

Q: *I am concerned about being seen at these meetings and people talking about me because I have been there. How private is a twelve-step, sexual-recovery meeting?*

A: While it is true that the meetings are not bound to the same level of confidentiality as a therapy group, all participants of twelve-step programs are committed to anonymity as a part of their own healing process. Many sex and love addiction recovery meetings are "closed," meaning they are available only to sex and love addicts, which adds an extra layer of safety. In almost every case, the benefits of attending a meeting far outweigh the possible negative consequences. And remember, people who see you there don't want to be talked about outside the meeting any more than you do.

Q: *I don't want to have to talk about myself publicly. Will they make me do this?*

A: Other than introducing yourself by your first name only, participation in twelve-step meetings is entirely voluntary. No one will make you talk about anything that you don't wish to divulge.

Q: *I have heard that a lot of freaks and sex offenders go to these meetings. Is that true? My problems haven't really hurt anybody other than myself, and I don't think I will feel comfortable around a bunch of sex offenders.*

A: A wide range of people attend sex and love addiction twelve-step recovery meetings, from those who are court-mandated to those whose behaviors harm no one but themselves. Believe it or not, there is something to be gained from hearing almost everyone's story at the meetings. At the end of each meeting, you can decide whom you would like to get to know better and whose example you want to follow.

Q: *I have heard that there is a lot of emphasis in these meetings on religion. I don't feel comfortable with all that God stuff, and I certainly don't want to trade my sexual problems for being involved in a cult. What's the deal with this?*

A: Twelve-step groups are definitely not cults. They do, however, use phrases like "higher power," and "a power greater than ourselves," to help addicts put their faith in something beyond their own best thinking. The word "God" is used as well, usually followed by the words "as we understand God," creating a lot of leeway for those who struggle with organized religion and the "God of their childhood." The reference to "God" in the Twelve Steps is not in any way directed toward a specific religion or belief system.

Q: *I hear that more people get picked up for sex in those meetings than actually get well. Is that true?*

A: If your goal is finding sex, you probably know by now that you can pretty much find it anywhere. If you go to a twelve-step meeting looking for the support of people who have long periods of sexual healing—people who can and will lend you a helping hand—then that is what you will find. If you go to a twelve-step meeting in hookup mode, you may be able to persuade someone to be sexual with you. In general, however, the meetings are safe, supportive places. That said, it is always best to get together with new members only in public, staying at the meeting places or perhaps a coffee shop. It is also best to avoid getting too involved with one member too quickly, as intense relationships are often a hallmark of sexual and romantic addiction.

Q: *What is a sponsor and how do I choose one?*

A: Sponsors are personal guides to healing and staying sober, usually not friends to begin with and *never* lovers. Typically, a sponsor is someone of the same gender who has been in recovery long enough to have achieved some success. He or she should be active in the recovery meetings and have worked through the Twelve Steps. In addition, a sponsor's personal situation should somewhat match your own so that he or she can help guide you more individually. For example, if you are married with kids, a sponsor who is also married with kids might be preferable. If you are HIV-positive, it might be helpful to have an HIV-positive sponsor. You choose a sponsor by listening to various people at meetings until you hear someone whose message resonates with you. When you find someone you connect with, you simply approach that person before or after a meeting and ask, "Are you available to be a sponsor and, if so, would you like to have coffee and hear my story?"

This is the best way to start. If that person says no, don't take it personally or give up (you don't know where they are on their recovery journey); just ask someone else.

Faith-Based Support Groups

Twelve-step groups are spiritual programs, but not religious. For people to whom a specific religion is important, there are multiple faith-based resources and strategies for healing. These can be used in conjunction with or separate from individual therapy, group therapy, and twelve-step programs. (Twelve-step programs are compatible with any religion.) Happily, there are many well-constructed and well-run faith-based recovery groups for sex and love addicts. The best of these programs focus on shame reduction, peer support, accountability, and hope.

I do not recommend faith-based programs that attempt to alter a sex addict's behavior by shaming the person, or by insisting that prayer and spiritual study, in and of themselves, will fix the problem and eliminate the sexual acting out. Fortunately, many faith-based programs today are non-shaming, accountability-based, and highly supportive—recognizing that sex and love addicts are not "morally challenged people" who lack the willpower needed to control their sexual and romantic behaviors, but people dealing with serious emotional and psychological pain who need empathetic support and direction.

Basic Information About Interventionists

Once upon a time, interventionists focused almost completely on getting an addict into inpatient treatment. Little thought was given to the needs of the addict's family, or to the addict's post-rehab care.

In recent years, however, intervention specialists have learned two very important lessons:

1) Addiction is a family disease, and if the entire family is not educated and (if/when necessary) treated, then the addict's odds of relapse increase significantly. In other words, if the addict returns from inpatient treatment to the same exact environment that triggered and enabled his or her addiction in the first place, relapse is likely.

2) There is no cure for addiction. Instead, like other chronic diseases, remission involves a lifelong effort. People with diabetes must watch what they eat, monitor their insulin levels, and perhaps take medication for life. If they fail to do so, their disease will get worse. And usually that occurs relatively rapidly. *Sex addiction is the same.* Recovery is a lifelong process.

Recognizing these facts, interventionists have become much more expansive in terms of the services they offer, with family care and long-term follow-up generally a part of the package. Many interventionists will also travel to the inpatient treatment facility with the addict, ensuring that he or she actually arrives and checks in. And nearly all interventionists are active in the addict's aftercare planning, helping to pick a proper outpatient therapist for continued treatment, and even advising about which twelve-step meetings to attend.

Unsurprisingly, given the comprehensive nature of the modern-day intervention process, these services can be expensive. Generally, a proper intervention costs at least $2,000, and usually the price is closer to $5,000. That said, for those who can afford it, interventionists can be very helpful. To find a good sexual-addiction interventionist, seek referrals from any CSAT-certified therapist. (CSATs can be located via the website of the International Institute for Trauma and Addictions Professionals, based on your town/zip code, at: *www.sexhelp.com* and *www.iitap.com*. More info about these sites to follow.)

Twelve-Step Groups

Sex Addicts Anonymous (SAA), 800-477-8191; 713-869-4902, *saa-recovery .org*

Sex and Love Addicts Anonymous (SLAA), 210-828-7900, *slaafws.org*

Sexaholics Anonymous (SA), 866-424-8777, *sa.org*

Sexual Compulsives Anonymous (SCA), 800-977-HEAL, *sca-recovery.org*

Sexual Recovery Anonymous (SRA), *sexualrecovery.org*

General Information

Websites for general support and information include:

The Relativity Website (*sexualrecovery.com*) has extensive information about dealing with and healing from sexual addiction, love addiction, and other intimacy disorders.

The American Association of Sexuality Educators, Counselors, and Therapists website (*aasect.org*) offers a great deal of useful information for cybersex addicts.

The Association for the Treatment of Sexual Abusers website (*atsa.com*) offers useful information about sexual abuse.

The Ben Franklin Institute offers, live, online and DVD trainings that can be accessed via their website (*bfisummit.com*). Much of author Rob Weiss's material has been recorded by them and is available for purchase.

The International Institute for Trauma & Addiction Professionals (*iitap. com*) has contact information for therapists, listed by state, who are certified as CSATs (Certified Sex Addiction Therapists).

Robert Weiss's website (*robertweissmsw.com*) has extensive information about dealing with and healing from sexual addiction, love addiction, and other intimacy disorders.

The Safer Society Foundation website (*safersociety.org*) offers useful information on sexual abuse.

Dr. Patrick Carnes' website (*sexhelp.com*) offers a great deal of useful information for sex addicts.

The Society for the Advancement of Sexual Health website (*sash.net*) provides contact information for knowledgeable therapists, listed by city and state, as well as information about upcoming sex-addiction conferences and training events.

Recommended Reading

Answers in the Heart: Daily Meditations for Men and Women Recovering from Sex Addiction (Anonymous)

Sex Addicts Anonymous (Anonymous)

Sex and Love Addicts Anonymous (Anonymous)

Contrary to Love: Helping the Sexual Addict by Dr. Patrick Carnes

Don't Call It Love: Recovery from Sex Addiction by Dr. Patrick Carnes

A Gentle Path through the Twelve Steps: A Guide for All People in the Process of Recovery by Dr. Patrick Carnes

Out of the Shadows: Understanding Sex Addiction by Dr. Patrick Carnes

Breaking the Cycle: Free Yourself from Sex Addiction, Porn Obsession, and Shame by George Collins and Andrew Adelman

Disclosing Secrets: An Addict's Guide for When, to Whom, and How Much to Reveal by Dr. M. Deborah Corley and Dr. Jennifer Schneider

No Stones: Women Redeemed from Sexual Addiction by Marnie Ferree

Understanding and Treating Sex Addiction: A Comprehensive Guide for People Who Struggle with Sex Addiction and Those Who Want to Help Them by Paula Hall

Ready to Heal: Breaking Free of Addictive Relationships by Kelly McDaniel

Always Turned On: Sex Addiction in the Digital Age by Robert Weiss and Dr. Jennifer Schneider

Cruise Control: Understanding Sex Addiction in Gay Men (2nd edition) by Robert Weiss

Basic Resources for Loved Ones of Addicts

Twelve-Step Groups

Adult Children of Alcoholics, 310-534-1815, *adultchildren.org*

Al-Anon, 888-425-2666, *al-anon.org*

Alateen (ages twelve to seventeen), 757-563-1600, *al-anon.org/for-alateen*

Co-Anon, 480-442-3869, *co-anon.org*

Co-Dependents Anonymous (CoDA), 888-444-2359, *coda.org*

Co-Dependents of Sex Addicts (COSA), 866-899-2672, *cosa-recovery.org*

Families Anonymous, 800-736-9805, *familiesanonymous.org*

Recovering Couples Anonymous, 877-663-2317, *recovering-couples.org*

S-Anon, 800-210-8141, 615-833-3152, *sanon.org*

Recommended Reading

Codependents' Guide to the Twelve Steps by Melody Beatty

Codependent No More: How to Stop Controlling Others and Start Caring for Yourself by Melody Beattie

Open Hearts: Renewing Relationships with Recovery, Romance, & Reality by Dr. Patrick Carnes, Debra Laaser, and Mark Laaser

Mending a Shattered Heart: A Guide for Partners of Sex Addicts by Dr. Stefanie Carnes

A Couple's Guide to Sexual Addiction: A Step-by-Step Plan to Rebuild Trust and Restore Intimacy by Paldrom Collins and George Collins

Surviving Disclosure: A Partner's Guide for Healing the Betrayal of Intimate Trust by Dr. M. Deborah Corley and Dr. Jennifer Schneider

Forgiveness: Finding Peace Through Letting Go by Adam Hamilton and Rob Simbeck

For Love and Money: Exploring Sexual & Financial Betrayal in Relationships by Debra Kaplan

Facing Codependence: What It Is, Where It Comes From, How It Sabotages Our Lives by Pia Mellody, Andrea Wells Miller, and J. Keith Miller

Sex, Lies, and Forgiveness (3rd edition) by Dr. Jennifer Schneider and Burt Schneider

Back from Betrayal: Recovering from His Affairs (3rd edition) by Dr. Jennifer Schneider

Forgiveness: Overcoming the Impossible by Matthew West

Forgiveness: 21 Days to Forgive Everyone for Everything by Iyanla Vanzart

Basic Resources for Addicts

Twelve-Step Groups

Alcoholics Anonymous, 212-870-3400, *aa.org*

Cocaine Anonymous, 310-559-5833, 800-347-8998, *ca.org*

Crystal Meth Anonymous, 855-638-4373, *crystalmeth.org*

Debtors Anonymous, 800-421-2383, *debtorsanonymous.org*

Food Addicts Anonymous, 772-878-9657, *foodaddictsanonymous.org*

Food Addicts in Recovery Anonymous, 781-932-6300, *foodaddicts.org*

Gamblers Anonymous, 626-960-3500, *gamblersanonymous.org/ga*

Marijuana Anonymous, 800-766-6779, *marijuana-anonymous.org*

Narcotics Anonymous, 818-773-9999, *na.org*

Nicotine Anonymous, 877-879-6422, *nicotine-anonymous.org*

Online Gamers Anonymous, 612-245-1115, *olganon.org*

Overeaters Anonymous, 505-891-2664, *oa.org*

Pills Anonymous, *pillsanonymous.org*

Spenders Anonymous, *spenders.org*

Workaholics Anonymous, 510-273-9253, *workaholics-anonymous.org*

General Information

The Mayo Clinic offers great information about compulsive gambling: what
it is, how to recognize it, how it can be treated, and so on on their website:
*mayoclinic.org/diseases-conditions/compulsive-gambling/basics/definition/
con-20023242.*

Useful information on compulsive spending can be found at *ncbi.nlm.nih
.gov/pmc/articles/PMC1805733/.*

Useful information on digital and online video game addiction can be found
at *video-game-addiction.org.*

Useful information about all types of eating disorders can be found on the
National Eating Disorders Association website at *nationaleatingdisorders.
org/.*

General information about substance abuse and mental health can be found on the Substance Abuse and Mental Health Services Administration website at *samhsa.gov/*.

General information on substance abuse can be found on the National Council on Alcoholism and Drug Dependence website at *ncadd.org/*.

General information on substance abuse can be found on the National Institute on Drug Abuse website at *drugabuse.gov/*.

Some of the specific private treatment centers that provide solid substance abuse treatment are quite well known, such as the Betty Ford Center, Promises or Hazelden. Another good place to look is at Elements Behavioral Health programs, *elementsbehavioralhealth.com/treatment/*.

> Note that treatment programs ("rehab" centers) are often only as good as the staff working there and the program they are running—today. So it is important to get a variety of opinions and feedback on where might be best place to consider (this means looking not only online, where such information can be deceptive at times, but also talking to real people). Addiction specialists, social workers, and most mental-health professionals have treatment centers they prefer for differing reasons with differing populations, so the more information you can gather before making a decision, the better.

Recommended Reading

8 Keys to Recovery from an Eating Disorder: Effective Strategies from Therapeutic Practice and Personal Experience by Carolyn Costin and Gwen Schubert Grabb

Alcoholics Anonymous (Anonymous)

Bought Out and Spent! Recovery from Compulsive Shopping and Spending by Terrence Schulman

Change Your Gambling, Change Your Life: Strategies for Managing Your Gambling and Improving Your Finances, Relationships, and Health by Dr. Howard Shaffer

Cyber Junkie: Escape the Gaming and Internet Trap by Kevin Roberts

Facing Addiction: Starting Recovery from Alcohol and Drugs by Dr. Patrick Carnes, Dr. Stefanie Carnes, and Dr. John Bailey

A Gentle Path through the Twelve Steps: A Guide for All People in the Process of Recovery by Dr. Patrick Carnes

Gripped by Gambling by Marilyn Lancelot

Healing Your Hungry Heart: Recovering from Your Eating Disorder by Joanna Poppink

Hooked on Games: The Lure and Cost of Video Game and Internet Addiction by Andrew Doan, Brooke Strickland, and Douglas Gentile

Living Sober (Anonymous)

A Man's Way through the Twelve Steps by Dan Griffin

Narcotics Anonymous (Anonymous)

Overcoming Your Pathological Gambling: Workbook by Robert Ladouceur and Stella Lachance

Spent: Break the Buying Obsession and Discover Your True Worth by Dr. Sally Palaian

To Buy or Not to Buy: Why We Overshop, and How to Stop by Dr. April Benson

Twelve Steps and Twelve Traditions (Anonymous)

Twenty-Four Hours a Day (Anonymous)

A Woman's Way through the Twelve Steps by Dr. Stephanie Covington

17

Bonus Chapter for Therapists: The Unofficial Diagnosis of Sexual Addiction

In the spring of 2013, the American Psychiatric Association (APA) published the latest edition of its *Diagnostic and Statistical Manual of Mental Disorders* (the DSM-5) without listing sexual addiction as an official diagnosis. Because the DSM-5 is the unofficial "diagnostic bible" used by the vast majority of treatment providers and insurance companies, this exclusion is significant. Yes, sex addicts can still be self-identified and/or clinically diagnosed as sexually addicted, but when they seek insurance-funded professional help they often run into problems because insurance companies typically won't pay for treatment without an officially sanctioned DSM-5 diagnosis. As a result, sex addicts and those who treat them must sometimes work around the APA's currently flawed system, usually by listing a related or a co-occurring issue—depression, anxiety, substance abuse, an eating disorder, etc.—as the primary reason for treatment. Needless to say, this is less than ideal.

Amazingly, sexual addiction (sometimes referred to as Hyper-sexual Disorder) was omitted from the DSM-5, despite an APA-commissioned position paper prepared by Dr. Martin Kafka of Harvard Medical School that recommended inclusion. Dr. Kafka wrote:

> THE DATA REVIEWED FROM THESE VARYING theoretical perspectives is compatible with the formulation that Hypersexual Disorder is a sexual desire disorder characterized by an increased frequency and intensity of sexually motivated fantasies, arousal, urges, and enacted behavior in association with an impulsivity component—a maladaptive behavioral response with adverse consequences. Hypersexual Disorder can be associated with vulnerability to dysphoric affects and the use of sexual behavior in response to dysphoric affects and/or life stressors associated with such affects. . . . Hypersexual Disorder is associated with increased time engaging in sexual fantasies and behaviors (sexual preoccupation/sexual obsession) and a significant degree of volitional impairment or "loss of control" characterized as disinhibition, impulsivity, compulsivity, or behavioral addiction. . . . [Hypersexual Disorder] can be accompanied by both clinically significant personal distress and social and medical morbidity.[1]

Though Dr. Kafka's language is somewhat technical, his message is clear: sexual addiction is a very real and debilitating psychiatric condition. Recognizing this, Dr. Kafka proposed specific diagnostic criteria for adoption by the APA. Essentially, his suggested criteria are as follows:

Hypersexual Disorder occurs when, over a period of at least six months, sexual fantasies, urges, and behaviors occur in association with three or more of the following:

- ✓ Interference with other important (nonsexual) goals, activities, and obligations
- ✓ Dysphoric mood states (anxiety, depression, irritability, etc.)
- ✓ Use as a coping mechanism (to avoid/not feel stress, emotional discomfort, physical discomfort, etc.)
- ✓ Repeated but unsuccessful efforts to control the fantasies, urges and behaviors
- ✓ Continued fantasies, urges and behaviors despite negative consequences

With his position paper, Dr. Kafka confirmed what sex addicts and sexual addiction treatment specialists have known for decades: Sexual addiction is an obsessive, out-of-control pattern of sexual fantasy and behaviors that creates directly related negative life consequences, including relationship problems, trouble at work or in school, loss of interest in other activities/obligations, isolation, decreased self-esteem, financial woes, legal issues, etc. Dr. Kafka also noted that sexual addiction, like other addictions, is typically a maladaptive attempt to self-soothe and/or self-medicate stress and other forms of emotional discomfort, including the pain of unresolved psychiatric conditions like depression, anxiety, attachment disorders, and early-life or severe adult trauma.

So why did the APA exclude sexual addiction from the DSM-5? In the introduction to the Addictive Disorders section they write:

OTHER EXCESSIVE BEHAVIORAL PATTERNS, such as Internet gaming, have also been described, but the research on these and other behavioral syndromes is less clear. Thus, groups of repetitive

behaviors, which some term *behavioral addictions*, with such subcate-
gories as "sex addiction," "exercise addiction," or "shopping addiction,"
are not included because at this time there is insufficient peer-
reviewed evidence to establish the diagnostic criteria and course
descriptions needed to identify these behaviors as mental disorders.[2]

In reality, as Dr. Kafka rather eloquently detailed in his position
paper, there is more than enough evidence for the APA to officially
recognize Hypersexual Disorder. In fact, many of the disorders currently included in the DSM-5 (particularly the sex-related disorders)
have significantly less supportive evidence. On this topic Dr. Kafka
wrote: "The number of cases of Hypersexual Disorder reported in the
peer reviewed journals greatly exceeds the number of cases of some of
the codified paraphilic disorders, such as Fetishism and Frotteurism."[3]
Nevertheless, the APA opted for "lack of research" as support for its
obstinate, behind-the-times refusal to acknowledge sexual addiction.

Happily, new research on sex addiction emerges on a relatively
regular basis. Of the studies published post-Kafka, three are especially
important.

First we have a diagnostic criteria field trial.[4] The goal of this
research was to find out if people who seek treatment for sexual addiction are accurately identified by Dr. Kafka's proposed diagnosis, and,
at the same time, to make sure those who do not seek treatment for
hypersexuality are not misidentified as sex addicts. According to the
study, the proposed diagnostic criteria are well-constructed, accurately
identifying self-identified sex addicts while not misdiagnosing non-
sex addicts. Most notable is the fact that many of the study's subjects
who sought treatment for substance abuse also reported problematic
sexual activity, but only when drinking or using, and the proposed
diagnosis identified only one of those individuals as sexually addicted.
For the others, the primary diagnosis was substance addiction.

A second study looked at attentional bias[5]—i.e., the tendency of addicts to focus a higher-than-normal share of their attention on an addiction-related cue, which typically creates a slowed reaction and/or an incomplete recollection of a certain event. For example, drug addicts will, when they see drug-related stimuli, manifest an incomplete or slowed memory of surrounding but non-drug-related items and events. So if you put a cocaine addict in a room and there is a pile of white powder on the coffee table, the addict will recall the powder and the table quickly and easily, but he or she might not remember the color of the carpet at all. Over the years, numerous studies have linked attentional bias with substance addiction, but this study was the first to look at whether sex addicts display similar attentional bias (with sexual stimuli). Unsurprisingly, they do.

While the diagnostic field trial and the attentional bias research are useful support for a sexual addiction diagnosis, they are probably not enough to change the APA's stance. What has really been needed is definitive proof that sex addiction manifests in the brain in the same way as other addictions. And, with the third study, this proof recently arrived.[6] Using fMRI (functional magnetic resonance imaging) scans, researchers compared the brain activity of sex addicts to the brain activity of non-sex addicts, and also to the brain activity of drug addicts. Unsurprisingly, they found significant differences in the brain response manifested by sex addicts and non-sex addicts, and striking similarities in the brain response manifested by sex addicts and drug addicts. Put simply, the research team found that when sex addicts are shown pornography their brains activate in three primary areas—the amygdala, the dorsal anterior cingulate, and the ventral striatum (regions of the brain in charge of things like mood, anticipatory pleasure, memory, and decision-making)—while the brains of non-sex addicts do not. They further concluded that this activation closely mirrors the brain activity of drug addicts when they are exposed to drug-related stimuli. Needless to say, these findings are significant.

So is the APA likely to move forward with an addendum to the DSM-5 that officially recognizes sexual addiction as an identifiable and treatable disorder? Probably not anytime soon. When it comes to making significant changes to the ways in which clinicians view psychiatric disorders, the APA is nearly always the last to arrive at the party. That said, they will have to concede at some point because significant research is piling up, most notably the fMRI study cited above. In fact, one member of the APA committee that considered but ultimately rejected Hypersexual Disorder for inclusion in the DSM-5, Dr. Richard Krueger of Columbia University, has called the fMRI research a "seminal study" supporting an eventual sex-addiction diagnosis.[7] Until the APA alters its stance of willful ignorance, however, nothing much changes. Sex addicts hoping to heal will seek therapy and twelve-step recovery, and the clinicians who treat them will do so in the ways they know best, with or without APA recognition and support.

The Neurobiology of Limerence vs. Love

Sex and love addicts often want to know: what is the difference between limerence and love, and how are they related?

Happily, thanks to modern brain-imaging studies, this question is easily answered. Typically, these studies are conducted using fMRI (functional magnetic resonance imaging) technology, which allows researchers to measure brain activity in response to various stimuli. Essentially, when one portion of the brain is activated—by a thought, an emotion, a movement, or anything else—blood flow to and within that area increases, and fMRI scans clearly depict this. In this way, tracking what happens in the brain when an individual experiences things like sexual arousal and long-term love is a relatively straight-forward task.

One rather extensive study combined and analyzed the results of twenty separate fMRI trials looking at brain reactivity in response to physical attraction, sexual arousal, and long-term love.[8] After pooling this extensive data, scientists were able to "map" the ways in which both sexual desire and long-term love stimulate the brain. The two main findings were as follows:

1) Sexual desire and long-term love both stimulate the striatum, an area of the brain that includes the *nucleus accumbens* (the rewards center). This means that both sexual attraction and lasting love create the experience of pleasure.

2) Long-term love (but *not* sexual desire) also stimulates the insula, an area of the brain associated with motivation. In other words, the insula "gives value" to pleasurable and/or life-sustaining activities (to make sure we continue to engage in them). This means that lasting love has an inherent "value" that sexual attraction does not.

In short, the striatum (the home of the rewards center) is responsible for initial attraction and sexual desire, i.e., limerence, while the *insula* is responsible for transforming that desire into long-term love.

Interestingly, the striatum is the area of the brain most closely associated with the formation of addiction. In fact, addictive substances and activities all rather thoroughly stimulate this segment of the brain. As such, it is hardly surprising that some people (i.e., love addicts) might get hooked on the limerence stage of relationships. After all, limerence produces the same basic high (the same basic neurobiological stimulation) as cocaine, heroin, sexual activity, gambling, and other addictive substances and behaviors: the release of dopamine, adrenaline, oxytocin, serotonin, and various other endorphins.

One very interesting facet of the above findings is that the striatum, the portion of the brain most closely associated with addiction, *must be stimulated* if a person wishes to build and maintain long-term love. In fact, this neurobiological rush is what pushes couples toward the slow and steady development of mature intimacy and longer-term relationships. This means that *limerence, the addiction-like stage of a romantic relationship, is a necessary step on the road to long-term love.* As such, even healthy relationships can look a lot like love addiction in the early stages. Of course, the difference between love addicts and healthy people is that love addicts never make it past limerence; they never "assign value" to anything beyond the initial intensity they experience. Instead, they seek to continually stimulate their brain's pleasure center with one new relationship after another, just as alcoholics stimulate their brains with one drink after another, and sex addicts repeatedly stimulate their brains with sexual fantasies, images, and encounters.

NOTES

Chapter 1

1 American Psychiatric Association (2013). *Diagnostic and statistical manual of mental disorders: DSM-5,* p 481. Washington, D.C.: American Psychiatric Association.

2 American Psychiatric Association (2013). *Diagnostic and statistical manual of mental disorders: DSM-5,* pp 481–584. Washington, D.C.: American Psychiatric Association.

3 American Psychiatric Association (2013). *Diagnostic and statistical manual of mental disorders: DSM-5,* pp 585–589. Washington, D.C.: American Psychiatric Association.

4 "Definition of Addiction," American Society of Addiction Medicine, accessed Dec 31, 2014, asam.org/for-the-public/definition-of-addiction.

5 National Institute on Drug Abuse. (2007). Drugs, brains, and behavior: The science of addiction. Retrieved September 3, 2014, from *drugabuse.gov/publications/topics-in-brief/drugs-brains-behavior-science-addiction*; Clay, S. W. (2010). Risk factors for addiction. *Osteopathic Family Physician, 2*(2), 41–45; and numerous other studies.

6 American Psychiatric Association (2013). *Diagnostic and statistical manual of mental disorders: DSM-5,* pp 235-264. Washington, D.C.: American Psychiatric Association.

7 Hall, P. (2013). *Understanding and treating sex addiction: A comprehensive guide for people who struggle with sex addiction and those who want to help them,* p 15. London: Routledge.

8 Carnes, P. (2001). *Out of the shadows: Understanding sexual addiction* (3rd Ed.). Center City, MN: Hazelden.

9 Hall, P. (2013). *Understanding and treating sex addiction: A comprehensive guide for people who struggle with sex addiction and those who want to help them,* pp 51–60. London: Routledge.

10 Carnes, P. (1983). *Out of the shadows: Understanding sexual addiction* (1st Edition). Center City, MN: Hazelden.

11 American Psychological Association. "Sexual orientation and homosexuality," apa.org/helpcenter/, accessed Jan 7, 2015.

12 American Psychiatric Association. (2013). *Diagnostic and statistical manual of mental disorders, (DSM-5),* p 686. American Psychiatric Pub.

13 American Psychiatric Association. (2013). *Diagnostic and statistical manual of mental disorders, (DSM-5).* American Psychiatric Pub.

Chapter 2

1 Carnes, P. (1991). *Don't call it love: Recovery from sexual addiction.* New York, NY: Bantam Books.

Chapter 3

1 Everitt, B. J., & Robbins, T. W. (2005). Neural systems of reinforcement for drug addiction: From actions to habits to compulsion. *Nature neuroscience, 8*(11), 1481–1489.

2 Volkow, N. D., Fowler, J. S., Wang, G. J., Swanson, J. M., & Telang, F. (2007). Dopamine in drug abuse and addiction: Results of imaging studies and treatment implications. *Archives of neurology, 64*(11), 1575–1579; Kenny, P. J., Voren, G., & Johnson, P. M. (2013). Dopamine D2 receptors and striatopallidal transmission in addiction and obesity. *Current opinion in neurobiology, 23*(4), 535–538; and Kühn, S., & Gallinat, J. (2014). Brain structure and functional connectivity associated with pornography consumption: the brain on porn. *JAMA psychiatry, 71*(7), 827–834.

3 Blum, K., Braverman, E. R., Holder, J. M., Lubar, J. F., Monastra, V. J., Miller, D., & Comings, D. E. (2000). The reward deficiency syndrome: A biogenetic model for the diagnosis and treatment of impulsive, addictive and compulsive behaviors. *Journal of Psychoactive Drugs, 32*(sup1), 1–112, and, Duvauchelle, C. L., Ikegami, A., & Castaneda, E. (2000). Conditioned increases in behavioral activity and accumbens dopamine levels produced by intravenous cocaine. *Behavioral neuroscience, 114*(6), 1156.

4 Hyman, S. E. (2005). Addiction: a disease of learning and memory. *Addiction, 162*(8); Hyman, S. E., & Malenka, R. C. (2001). Addiction and the brain: the neurobiology of compulsion and its persistence. *Nature reviews neuroscience, 2*(10), 695–703; and numerous other studies.

5 Carnes, P. J., Murray, R. E., & Charpentier, L. (2005). Bargains with chaos: Sex addicts and addiction interaction disorder. *Sexual Addiction & Compulsivity, 12*(2–3), 79-120; and Rosenberg, K. P., Carnes, P., & O'Connor, S. (2014). Evaluation and treatment of sex addiction. *Journal of sex & marital therapy, 40*(2), 77–91.

6 Rosenberg, K. P., Carnes, P., & O'Connor, S. (2014). Evaluation and treatment of sex addiction. *Journal of sex & marital therapy, 40*(2), 77–91.

Chapter 4

1 Schuckit, M. A., & Smith, T. L. (1996). An 8-year follow-up of 450 sons of alcoholic and control subjects. *Archives of General Psychiatry, 53*(3), 202–210.

2 Comings, D. E., Muhleman, D., Ahn, C., Gysin, R., & Flanagan, S. D. (1994). The dopamine D$_2$ receptor gene: a genetic risk factor in substance abuse. *Drug and alcohol dependence, 34*(3), 175–180, and, Comings, D. E., Ferry, L., Bradshaw-Robinson, S., Burchette, R., Chiu, C., & Muhleman, D. (1996). The dopamine D2 receptor (DRD2) gene: a genetic risk factor in smoking. *Pharmacogenetics and Genomics, 6*(1), 73–79, among other studies.

3 Thomasson, H. R., Edenberg, H. J., Crabb, D. W., Mai, X. L., Jerome, R. E., Li, T. K., ... & Yin, S. J. (1991). Alcohol and aldehyde dehydrogenase genotypes and alcoholism in Chinese men. *American journal of human genetics, 48*(4), 677, and, Crabb, D. W., Edenberg, H. J., Bosron, W. F., & Li, T. K. (1989). Genotypes for aldehyde dehydrogenase deficiency and alcohol sensitivity. The inactive ALDH2 (2) allele is dominant. *Journal of Clinical Investigation, 83*(1), 314, among other studies.

4 Goldman, D., Oroszi, G., & Ducci, F. (2005). The genetics of addictions: uncovering the genes. *Nature Reviews Genetics, 6*(7), 521–532, and, Kreek, M. J., Nielsen, D. A., Butelman, E. R., & LaForge, K. S. (2005). Genetic influences on impulsivity, risk taking, stress responsivity and vulnerability to drug abuse and addiction. *Nature neuroscience, 8*(11), 1450–1457, among other studies.

5 Levin, F. R., & Hennessy, G. (2004). Bipolar disorder and substance abuse. *Biological psychiatry, 56*(10), 738–748.

6 Goldman, D., Oroszi, G., & Ducci, F. (2005). The genetics of addictions: uncovering the genes. *Nature Reviews Genetics, 6*(7), 521–532.

7 Wolff, G. L., Kodell, R. L., Moore, S. R., & Cooney, C. A. (1998). Maternal epigenetics and methyl supplements affect agouti gene expression in Avy/a mice. *The FASEB Journal, 12*(11), 949–957, and, Cooney, C. A., Dave, A. A., & Wolff, G. L. (2002). Maternal methyl supplements in mice affect epigenetic variation and DNA methylation of offspring. *The Journal of nutrition, 132*(8), 2393S–2400S, among other studies.

8 Sigvardsson, S., Bohman, M., & Cloninger, C. R. (1996). Replication of the Stockholm Adoption Study of alcoholism: Confirmatory cross-fostering analysis. *Archives of General Psychiatry, 53*(8), 681–687, and, Goodwin, D. W. (1979). Alcoholism and heredity: A review and hypothesis. *Archives of General Psychiatry, 36*(1), 57–61, among other studies.

9 Kendler, K. S., Jacobson, K. C., Prescott, C. A., & Neale, M. C. (2003). Specificity of genetic and environmental risk factors for use and abuse/dependence of cannabis, cocaine, hallucinogens, sedatives, stimulants, and opiates in male twins. *American Journal of Psychiatry, 160*(4), 687–695, and, Agrawal, A., & Lynskey, M. T. (2008). Are there genetic influences on addiction: evidence from family, adoption and twin studies. *Addiction, 103*(7), 1069–1081, among other studies.

10 Anda, R., Felitti, V., Bremner, J., Walker, J., Whitfield, C., Perry, B., ... Giles, W. (2006). The enduring effects of abuse and related adverse experiences in childhood. *European Archives of Psychiatry and Clinical Neuroscience, 256*(3):174–186.

11 DeWit, D. J., Adlaf, E. M., Offord, D. R., & Ogborne, A. C. (2000). Age at first alcohol use: a risk factor for the development of alcohol disorders. *American Journal of Psychiatry, 157*(5), 745–750, and, Grant, B. F., Stinson, F. S., & Harford, T. C. (2001). Age at onset of alcohol use and DSM-IV alcohol abuse and dependence: a 12-year follow-up. *Journal of substance abuse, 13*(4), 493–504, among other studies.

12 Carnes, P. (1991). *Don't call it love: Recovery from sexual addiction.* New York, NY: Bantam.

13 Hall, P. (2013). Understanding and treating sex addiction: A comprehensive guide for people who struggle with sex addiction and those who want to help them, p 40. London: Routledge.

14 Wolak, J., Mitchell, K., & Finkelhor, D. (2007). Unwanted and wanted exposure to online pornography in a national sample of youth Internet users. *Pediatrics, 119*(2), 247–257.

15 Courtois, C. (2014). *It's not you, it's what happened to you,* p 5. Long Beach, CA: Elements Behavioral Health.

16 Courtois, C. A. & Ford, J. D. (Eds.). (2009). *Treating complex traumatic stress disorders: An evidence-based guide.* New York: Guilford, and, Yehuda, R. (2004). Risk and resilience in posttraumatic stress disorder. *Journal of Clinical Psychiatry, 65*(Supplement 1):29–36.

17 Courtois, C. A. & Ford, J. D. (Eds.) (2009). Treating complex traumatic stress disorders: An evidence-based guide. New York: Guilford, and, Ford, J. D. & Courtois, C. A. (2013). Treating complex traumatic stress disorders in children and adolescents: Scientific foundations and therapeutic models. New York: Guilford Press, and, Kira, I.A. (2010). Etiology and treatment of post-cumulative traumatic stress disorders in different cultures. Traumatology, (4):128–141.

18 Ford, J. D. (2009). Neurobiological and developmental research: clinical implications. In C. A. Courtois & J. D. Ford (Eds.), *Treating complex traumatic stress disorders: An evidence-based guide* (pp. 31–58). New York: Guilford Press.

19 Carnes, P. (1991). *Don't call it love: Recovery from sexual addiction.* New York, NY: Bantam.

20 Hall, P. (2013). *Understanding and treating sex addiction: A comprehensive guide for people who struggle with sex addiction and those who want to help them,* p 43. London: Routledge.

21 Ford, J. D. (2009). Neurobiological and developmental research: clinical implications. In C. A. Courtois & J. D. Ford (Eds.), *Treating complex traumatic stress disorders: An evidence-based guide* (pp. 31–58). New York: Guilford Press.

22 Adams, K. (2011). *Silently seduced, revised and updated: When parents make their children partners.* Deerfield Beach, FL: Health Communications, Incorporated.

23 Courtois, C. A. & Ford, J. D. (Eds.). (2009). *Treating complex traumatic stress disorders: An evidence-based guide*. New York: Guilford, and, Ford, J. D. & Courtois, C. A. (2013). *Treating complex traumatic stress disorders in children and adolescents: Scientific foundations and therapeutic models*. New York: Guilford Press.

24 Birchard, T. (2011). Sexual addiction and the paraphilias. *Sexual Addiction & Compulsivity, 18*(3), 157–187.

25 Adams, K. M. (2011). *Silently seduced: When parents make their children partners*. Health Communications, Inc.

26 Kaplan, D. (2012). "Emotional incest and the relationship avoidant." From debrakaplancounseling.com/emotional-incest-and-the-relationship-avoidant/, accessed Jan 23, 2015.

Chapter 5

1 Carnes, P. (1989). *Contrary to love: Helping the sexual addict*. Center City, MN: Hazelden.

2 A. Cooper, D. E. Putman, L. A. Planchon, and S. C. Boies, "Online Sexual Compulsivity: Getting Tangled in the Net," *Sexual Addiction and Compulsivity* 6 (1999): 79–104.

3 Ogas, O. & Gaddam, S. (2012). *A Billion Wicked Thoughts: What the Internet Tells Us About Sexual Relationships*. London: Plume.

4 Cooper, A. (1998). Sexuality and the Internet: Surfing into the new millennium. *CyberPsychology & Behavior, 1*(2), 187–193.

5 Vega, T. (2010, August 16). Dating Site Marks 10 Years. *New York Times*, p. B4.

6 Crook, J. (2015, January 12). Tinder Acquires Ephemeral Messenger Tappy. Retrieved March 25, 2015, from *techcrunch.com/2015/01/12/tinder-acquires-ephemeral-messenger-tappy/*

7 Damania, D. (2014). "Internet pornography statistics," *thedinfographics.com/2011/12/23/internet-pornography-statistics/*, accessed May 28, 2014.

8 Cooper, A. Putnam D.E., Planchon, A. & Boies, S.C. (1999). Online Sexual Compulsivity: Getting Tangled in the Net. *Sexual Addiction and* Compulsivity 6(2):79–104.

9 Hall, P. (2012). *Understanding and treating sex addiction: A comprehensive guide for people who struggle with sex addiction and those who want to help them*. Routledge.

10 Raymond, N. C., Coleman, E., & Miner, M. H. (2003). Psychiatric comorbidity and compulsive/impulsive traits in compulsive sexual behavior. *Comprehensive Psychiatry, 44*(5), 370–380.

11 Voon, V., Mole, T. B., Banca, P., Porter, L., Morris, L., Mitchell, S., & Irvine, M. (2014). Neural correlates of sexual cue reactivity in individuals with and without compulsive sexual behaviours. *PloS one, 9*(7), e102419.

12 Rosenberg, K. P., Carnes, P., & O'Connor, S. (2014). Evaluation and treatment of sex addiction. *Journal of sex & marital therapy, 40*(2), 77–91.

13 Wilson, G. (2014). *Your Brain on Porn: Internet Pornography and the Emerging Science of Addiction*. Richmond, VA: Commonwealth Publishing.

Chapter 6

1 Carnes, P. (1989). *Contrary to love: Helping the sexual addict*. Minneapolis, MN: CompCare.

2 Finkelhor, D., Hotaling, G., Lewis, I., & Smith, C. (1990). Sexual abuse in a national survey of adult men and women: Prevalence, characteristics, and risk factors. *Child abuse & neglect, 14*(1), 19–28, and, Finkelhor, D. (1991). Child sexual abuse. *Violence in America–a public health approach*, 79–94.

3 Gray, J. (1992). *Men are from Mars, women are from Venus: The classic guide to understanding the opposite sex*. New York: HarperCollins.

4 Ogas, O., & Gaddam, S. (2011). *A billion wicked thoughts: What the internet tells us about sexual relationships*, pp 71.72. New York: Plume.

Chapter 7

1 Ferree, M. (2012) *Making Advances: A Comprehensive Guide for Treating Female Sex and Love Addicts*, Royston, GA: Society for the Advancement of Sexual Health, and, McDaniel, K. (2008) *Ready to Heal: Women Facing Love, Sex and Relationship Addiction*, Carefree, AZ: Gentle Path Press.

2 Ferree, M. (2012) *Making Advances: A Comprehensive Guide for Treating Female Sex and Love Addicts*, Royston, GA: Society for the Advancement of Sexual Health, and, McDaniel, K. (2008) *Ready to Heal: Women Facing Love, Sex and Relationship Addiction*, Carefree, AZ: Gentle Path Press.

Chapter 8

1 American Psychological Association Help Center. Sexual orientation and homosexuality. Retrieved Feb 6, 2015 from *apa.org/helpcenter/*; and American Psychiatric Association. Therapies Focused on Attempts to Change Sexual Orientation (Reparative or Conversion Therapies). Retrieved Feb 6, 2015 from psychiatry.org/.

2 American Psychological Association Help Center. Sexual orientation and homosexuality. Retrieved Feb 6, 2015 from *apa.org/helpcenter/*.

3 Ryan, C., Russell, S. T., Huebner, D., Diaz, R., & Sanchez, J. (2010). Family acceptance in adolescence and the health of LGBT young adults. *Journal of Child and Adolescent Psychiatric Nursing, 23*(4), 205–213.

4 Cabaj, R.P. (1996). Substance abuse in gay men, lesbians and bisexuals. In R.P. Cabaj & T.S. Stein (Eds.), *The textbook of homosexuality and mental health.* Washington, DC: American Psychiatric Press; and Cochran, S., Ackerman, D., Mays, V., & Ross, M. (2004). Prevalence of non-medical drug use and dependence among homosexually active men and women in the US population. *Addiction, 99*(8), 989–998.

5 Carnes, P. J., Murray, R. E., & Charpentier, L. (2005). Bargains with chaos: Sex addicts and addiction interaction disorder. *Sexual Addiction & Compulsivity, 12*(2–3), 79–120.

Chapter 9

1 Carnes, P. J., Murray, R. E., & Charpentier, L. (2005). Bargains with chaos: Sex addicts and addiction interaction disorder. *Sexual Addiction & Compulsivity, 12*(2–3), 79–120.

2 Carnes, P. J., Murray, R. E., & Charpentier, L. (2005). Bargains with chaos: Sex addicts and addiction interaction disorder. *Sexual Addiction & Compulsivity, 12*(2–3), 79–120.

3 Hall, P. (2013). *Understanding and treating sex addiction: A comprehensive guide for people who struggle with sex addiction and those who want to help them*, p 186. London: Routledge.

4 Carnes, P. J., Murray, R. E., & Charpentier, L. (2005). Bargains with chaos: Sex addicts and addiction interaction disorder. *Sexual Addiction & Compulsivity, 12*(2–3), 79–120.

5 Gatewood, T. (2009). Attitudes and motivating factors for methamphetamine use among HIV+ men who have sex with men. Thesis presented to the Faculty of the School of Social Work, Cal State University, Los Angeles.

6 Cheng, W., Garfein, R., Semple, S., Strathdee, S., Zians, J., & Patterson, T. (2009). Differences in sexual risk behaviors among male and female HIV-seronegative heterosexual methamphetamine users. *The American Journal of Drug and Alcohol Abuse, 35*(5), 295–300.

7 Cheng, W., Garfein, R., Semple, S., Strathdee, S., Zians, J., & Patterson, T. (2010). Binge use and sex and drug use behaviors among HIV(-) heterosexual methamphetamine users in San Diego. *Substance Use & Misuse, 45*(1–2), 116–133.

Chapter 10

1 Sullivan, J. T., Sykora, K., Schneiderman, J., Naranjo, C. A., & Sellers, E. M. (1989). Assessment of alcohol withdrawal: the revised clinical institute withdrawal assessment for alcohol scale (CIWA-Ar). *British journal of addiction, 84*(11), 1353–1357.

Chapter 11

1 American Psychiatric Association (2013). *Diagnostic and statistical manual of mental disorders: DSM-5*. Washington, D.C.: American Psychiatric Association.

Chapter 12

1 Schneider, J. P., Weiss, R., & Samenow, C. (2012). Is it really cheating? Understanding the emotional reactions and clinical treatment of spouses and partners affected by cybersex infidelity. *Sexual Addiction & Compulsivity, 19*(1–2), 123–139.

2 Steffens, B. A., & Rennie, R. L. (2006). The traumatic nature of disclosure for wives of sexual addicts. *Sexual Addiction & Compulsivity, 13*(2–3), 247–267.

3 Jason, S., & Minwalla, O. (2008). *Sexual trauma model: Partner's reaction, addict's reaction.* Presented at the National Conference of the Society for the Advancement of Sexual Health (SASH) (APA Accredited Presentation); and Minwalla, O. (2011). *A new generation of sex addiction treatment: The sex addiction-induced trauma model for the treatment of sex addicts, partners, and the couple.* Presented at the National Conference of the Society for the Advancement of Sexual Health (SASH), (APA Accredited Presentation).

Chapter 14

1 Brown, B. (2012). *Daring greatly: How the courage to be vulnerable transforms the way we live, love, parent and lead*. London: Penguin.

2 Hemenover, S. H. (2003). The good, the bad, and the healthy: Impacts of emotional disclosure of trauma on resilient self-concept and psychological distress. *Personality and Social Psychology Bulletin, 29*(10), 1236–1244, among other studies.

3 Briere, J. N., & Scott, C. (2014). *Principles of trauma therapy: A guide to symptoms, evaluation, and treatment.* Sage Publications.

4 Briere, J. N., & Scott, C. (2014). *Principles of trauma therapy: A guide to symptoms, evaluation, and treatment.* Sage Publications.

Chapter 17

1 Kafka, M. (2010). Hypersexual disorder: A proposed diagnosis for DSM-V. *Archives of sexual behavior, 39*(2), 377–400.

2 American Psychiatric Association (2013). *Diagnostic and statistical manual of mental disorders: DSM-5*, p 481. Washington, D.C.: American Psychiatric Association.

3 Kafka, M. (2010). Hypersexual disorder: A proposed diagnosis for DSM-V. *Archives of sexual behavior, 39*(2), 377–400.

4 Reid, R. C., Carpenter, B. N., Hook, J. N., Garos, S., Manning, J. C., Gilliland, R., & Fong, T. (2012). Report of findings in a DSM-5 field trial for hypersexual disorder. *The journal of sexual medicine, 9*(11), 2868–2877.

5 Mechelmans, D. J., Irvine, M., Banca, P., Porter, L., Mitchell, S., Mole, T. B., & Voon, V. (2014). Enhanced attentional bias towards sexually explicit cues in individuals with and without compulsive sexual behaviours. *PloS one, 9*(8), e105476.

6 Voon, V., Mole, T. B., Banca, P., Porter, L., Morris, L., Mitchell, S., ... & Irvine, M. (2014). Neural correlates of sexual cue reactivity in individuals with and without compulsive sexual behaviours. *PloS one, 9*(7), e102419.

7 Berman, T. (2014). Sexual addiction may be real after all. *ABC News.* Retrieved Jan 15, 2015 from *abcnews. go.com/blogs/health/2014/07/11/sexual-addiction-may-be-real-after-all/.*

8 Cacioppo, S., Bianchi-Demicheli, F., Frum, C., Pfaus, J., & Lewis, J. (2012). The common neural bases between sexual desire and love: A multilevel kernel density fMRI analysis. *Journal of Sexual Medicine 9*(4):1048–1054.

ABOUT THE AUTHOR

Robert Weiss, LCSW, CSAT-S, is Senior Vice President of National Clinical Development for Elements Behavioral Health. In this capacity, he has established and overseen addiction and mental health treatment programs for more than a dozen high-end treatment facilities, including Promises Treatment Centers in Malibu and Los Angeles, The Ranch in rural Tennessee, and The Right Step in Texas. He was instrumental in integrating Dr. Brené Brown's Daring Way™ curriculum into the Elements system. Previously, he developed sexual addiction treatment programming for the Sexual Recovery Institute in Los Angeles and The Life Healing Center in New Mexico.

An internationally acknowledged clinician and author, he has served as a subject expert on the intersection of human intimacy and digital technology for multiple media outlets including the Oprah Winfrey Network, the *New York Times*, the *Los Angeles Times*, the *Daily Beast*, and CNN, among many others.

He is the author of several highly regarded books, including *Sex Addiction 101: A Basic Guide to Healing from Sex, Love, and Porn Addiction* and *Cruise Control: Understanding Sex Addiction in Gay*

Men. He has also co-authored, with Jennifer Schneider, MD, both *Closer Together, Further Apart: The Effect of Technology and the Internet on Parenting, Work, and Relationships* and *Always Turned On: Sex Addiction in the Digital Age.* He is a regular contributor to several pop and clinical websites, including *Psychology Today, Huffington Post, Psych Central, Counselor Magazine,* and *Addiction.com,* among others. For more information please visit his website at *robertweissmsw.com* or follow him on Twitter, @RobWeissMSW.